Turiya

The Ultimate Guide to Pure Consciousness, Hindu Philosophy, Samadhi, Shiva, and Shakti

Your Free Gift
(only available for a limited time)

Thanks for getting this book! If you want to learn more about various spirituality topics, then join Mari Silva's community and get a free guided meditation MP3 for awakening your third eye. This guided meditation mp3 is designed to open and strengthen ones third eye so you can experience a higher state of consciousness. Simply visit the link below the image to get started.

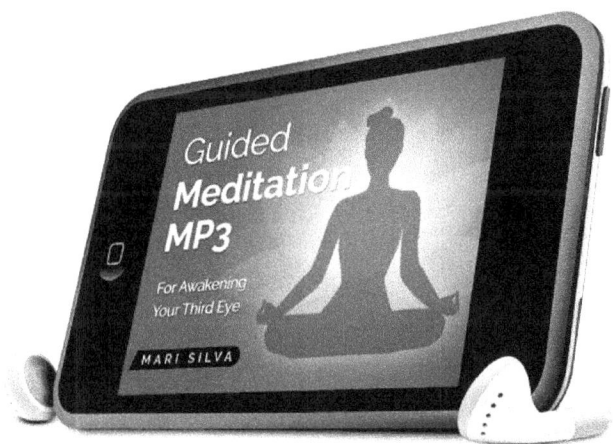

https://spiritualityspot.com/meditation

Table of Contents

Introduction

Have you ever known what it's like to experience a state of pure consciousness? Complete bliss and oneness with the universe? This is what the Hindus call turiya, or *pure consciousness.*

Hindu philosophy is based on the belief that one supreme reality pervades and underlies all creation. This supreme reality is called Brahman, and it is the ultimate goal of all spiritual seekers. Brahman is often described as an infinite, omnipresent, and eternal ocean of consciousness. It is the source of all things and the goal of all things. Everything that exists is a part of Brahman, and everything is striving to return to Brahman.

This comprehensive guide will explore turiya, how it relates to Hindu philosophy, and how you can experience it through yoga and meditation. We'll also provide some practical tips and techniques you can use to pave the way to this ultimate state of awareness.

But before we dive in, there are some basics that we need to cover. We'll talk about Shiva and Shakti, the two essential aspects of Brahman. These two concepts are often misunderstood, so it's crucial to clearly understand them before we move on. Next, we'll discuss Samadhi, the goal of all yoga and meditation practices. Once we clearly understand these concepts, we'll explore turiya in greater depth.

Turiya is a state of pure consciousness that is beyond all duality. It is the fourth and final state of consciousness in the Hindu tradition. The first three states are waking, dreaming, and deep sleep. Turiya is beyond all of these states. It is a state of pure awareness that is limitless. Turiya is often described as a state of complete bliss. It's a state of being at one with the universe. In this state, there is no sense of separation between the observer and the observed. There is no sense of I or me. There is only pure awareness.

So how do we experience this state of pure consciousness? The information in this guide will show you. In this easy-to-understand guide, you'll also find yoga sequences, meditation techniques, and mantras that will help you experience turiya for yourself. You'll also learn about the daily steps you can take to bring yourself closer to this state of pure consciousness. We'll also dispel some common myths about turiya so that you can approach this topic with clarity and understanding.

By the end of this guide, you'll clearly understand what turiya is and how you can experience it for yourself. You'll also have a toolkit of practical techniques that you can use to pave the way to this ultimate state of awareness. So let's get started!

Chapter 1: What Is Turiya, or Pure Consciousness?

Have you ever found yourself wondering what consciousness is? You're not alone. The great philosophers and spiritual thinkers throughout history have all dedicated themselves to trying to understand the nature of consciousness. And while there are many different theories out there, one of the most intriguing comes from the Hindu tradition.

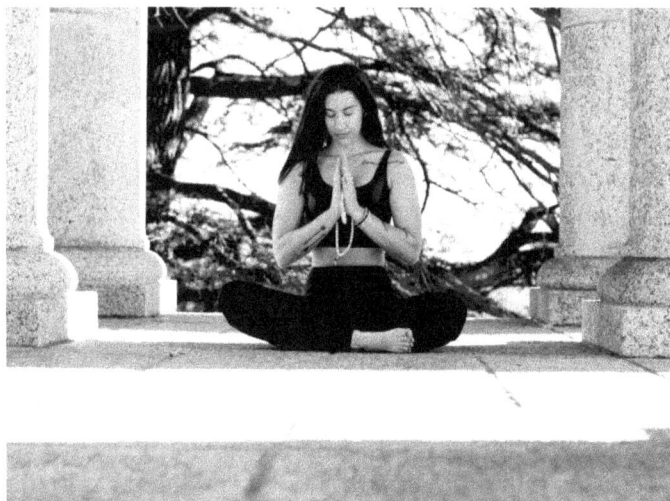

Turiya is described as the state of pure consciousness, the god state, or a great "cosmic silence."
https://www.pexels.com/photo/woman-in-black-tank-top-and-black-pants-sitting-on-concrete-floor-3820312/

In Hinduism, there is a concept known as turiya or pure consciousness. Its described as the state of pure consciousness, the god state, or a great "cosmic silence." To pave your way into thoroughly outlining what Turiya is, it might be best to first describe the four states of consciousness described by the Vedas and Upanishads: jagrata, svapna, susupti, and lastly, turiya.

This chapter will discuss the nature of consciousness according to Hinduism, focusing on the concept of turiya. We will explore how turiya is said to be different from the other three states of consciousness and how various Hindu traditions describe it. We will also look at accounts from gurus and experienced practitioners who have managed to access this state of pure consciousness. Finally, we will discuss how turiya has its stages.

The Four States of Consciousness

In the Hindu tradition, all humans regularly go through four distinct states of consciousness. The first of these is known as waking consciousness – when we are fully aware and awake. During this state, we experience life in full detail, interacting with our environment and taking in new information about the world around us. After a period of wakefulness comes dreaming, characterized by intense mental activity occurring while we sleep.

While our bodies rest, our minds continue to process information and generate ideas, creating vivid images and sensations. Next is deep sleep, or Susupti, which marks a phase where the mind rests completely. Finally, there is an even deeper state called Turiya – sometimes translated as 'pure awareness' – which involves an expanded state of consciousness that cannot be articulated entirely. Whether we are awake or asleep, these four states are an essential part of being human. Let's take a closer look at each one.

1. Jagrata: The Waking State

Jagrata, or "the waking state," is a concept that lies at the heart of Hinduism and other Indian spiritual traditions. In the jagrata state, one's awareness remains fully present in the body and attentive to the external world. Unlike in deep sleep or dreaming, a person in jagrata experiences complete lucidity, with all mental faculties functioning normally. Perhaps one of the key benefits of jagrata is that it gives rise to a clear understanding of one's own physical and mental limitations. By becoming more aware of how consciousness rises and subsides within us, we can develop mindfulness, which helps us to better navigate life's everyday challenges and experience greater peace and fulfillment. So whether you're seeking to deepen your spiritual practice or simply wish to live more mindfully, learning to stay in a state of jagrata may be just what you need.

2. Svapna: The Dreaming State

Svapna, or the dreaming state, has been another central concept in the two Hindu and Buddhist traditions for centuries. It refers to a state of mind in which one's consciousness separates from the physical body and travels freely through the spiritual realm. Some scholars claim this state can be induced through techniques such as yoga and meditation, while others believe that it will only occur spontaneously during sleep or intense spiritual practices. Regardless of its origins or mechanisms, many people view svapna as a powerful and transformative experience that offers insights into the nature of reality, self-knowledge, and enlightenment. Whether we fully understand it or not, svapna represents an essential part of our human experience, helping us to explore sides of ourselves that might otherwise remain hidden in our waking lives.

3. Susupti: The Deep Sleep State

Susupti is the Sanskrit word for a deep, dreamless sleep state. In this state, the body and mind fully relax and enter a state of complete rest. Though we may pass into susupti many times throughout the night as we sleep, it can also be experienced during moments of deep meditation or focus. Some scientists believe that the brain enters a strange kind of super-consciousness during these moments of susupti, allowing us to tap into our mental abilities in normally impossible ways. This may or may not be true, but there is no doubt that susupti holds great power and potential for anyone seeking greater levels of relaxation, inner peace, or insight. So why not take some time today to find your deep sleep state? With practice and patience, you will surely experience the incredible benefits of susupti for yourself.

4. Turiya: The State of Pure Consciousness

In many spiritual traditions, turiya is considered the ultimate state of consciousness. It's often described as a profound stillness that transcends all mental activity. In some ways, it can be thought of as a type of superconscious state where awareness is expanded to its fullest potential. Because it is beyond words or concepts, turiya can be difficult to fully grasp and understand. However, some have found that by cultivating certain techniques or practices, such as mindfulness or meditative techniques, one may eventually reach this extraordinary state of pure consciousness. Ultimately, turiya represents the ultimate goal of many aspiring seekers, beckoning us towards a deeper truth and harmony within ourselves.

Turiya beyond the Other Three States

Most traditions recognize that there is much more to consciousness than meets the eye. However, many traditions tend to focus on just one or two states at a time rather than exploring all aspects of consciousness in depth. While each state of consciousness is meaningful in its own right, it is also valuable to explore these states together, recognizing their interconnection and how they work together to create our overall experience. By doing so, we gain a deeper understanding of both ourselves and the world around us. And perhaps most importantly, we begin to realize that true enlightenment is not just about one particular state of mind; rather, it involves tapping into the full potential of human consciousness as a whole.

Ultimately, this limited perspective can hinder our spiritual development by limiting our perception of what lies beyond the other three states. To truly attain enlightenment - that is, to fully realize the potential of human consciousness - we must be willing and able to explore each dimension without attachment or aversion. Only then can we embark upon a truly transformative journey toward higher truth.

How Turiya Is Described in Various Hindu Traditions

Turiya, sometimes referred to as samadhi or ecstasy, is described very differently in various Hindu traditions. In Vedanta, turiya is described as a deep state of union with the divine, characterized by an overwhelming sense of timelessness and dissolution of individual identity. Maharishi Mahesh Yogi, one of the foremost yogic scholars of the 20th century, believed that turiya was attained through advanced meditation techniques and involved no cognitive awareness whatsoever. Conversely, Gaudapada and other members of the Shankara School describe turiya as more than just a spiritual state; they see it as a fundamental quality of reality itself. Regardless of the specific context in which it is discussed, one thing remains clear: turiya is profoundly transformative and has been revered throughout history by many different branches of Hinduism.

1. Vaishnavism

In the scriptures of Vaishnavism, turiya is a term often used to describe the ultimate state of spiritual awakening. This state represents a complete transcendence of all mental and sensory activity and is often equated with oneness with God. According to many Vaishnava texts, achieving this state requires intense dedication, deep begging practice, and constant devotion to the teachings of the sages. However, despite the challenges in attaining turiya, this state is believed to be attainable for anyone willing to put in the effort. With persistence and determination, even an ordinary person can achieve this greatly exalted spiritual state and experience true bliss. Ultimately, it can be said that turiya is one of the most precious gifts of Vaishnavism.

2. Shaivism

In the ancient Indian tradition of Shaivism, turiya is said to be the primordial energy and consciousness at the core of all existence. Often described as simultaneously transcendent and imminent, turiya is often conceived of as both formless and having a vast array of forms. With its immense powers, turiya is said to have created many aspects of reality, including universes, gods and goddesses, different levels of consciousness, and even sentient beings like humans and animals.

Not only is turiya seen as one of the most powerful forces in the universe, but it is also revered for its ability to awaken people's true potential. So, it's no surprise that many Shaivite practitioners strive to cultivate a close connection with this all-encompassing universal force. In essence, turiya can be thought of as the genesis of all that exists – both timeless and ever-changing, full of infinite wisdom yet bursting with endless creativity. Whether one connects with it through meditation, prayer, or other means, its power is undeniable, offering guidance and inspiration to anyone seeking it out.

3. Shaktism

In Shaktism, another tradition of Hinduism dedicated to the worship of the sacred feminine principle known as Shakti, turiya is often described as a divine force that permeates all aspects of the universe. This concept can be understood both spiritually and metaphysically. On the one hand, turiya is thought to manifest in sensory experience as an underlying presence that runs through all things, connecting them and infusing them with a sense of divinity. On the other hand, turiya also represents a transcendent state beyond the realm of duality and logic. In this sense, it points to a deeper reality that cannot be grasped by the mind or experienced with ordinary senses. Whether experienced on an individual or cosmic level, turiya is seen as essential for our understanding of life and the divine.

4. Smartism

In the tradition of Smartism, turiya is also often described as the highest spiritual state one can attain. This state represents a deep connection with one's true nature and opens up new realms of consciousness and understanding. To achieve this state, one must practice meditation and other forms of introspection daily. However, it is also essential to cultivate compassion for others, both human and non-human alike. By embracing turiya, we can find wisdom, peace, and freedom from suffering in our lives. Through this transformative process, we become more fully connected to the divine light within us all. While the path to reaching turiya may be long and challenging at times, it is worth every step along the way. Ultimately, turiya proves that our greatest power comes not from outside ourselves but from within ourselves.

5. The Vedas

In the Vedas, turiya is often described as an essential and sacred state of being. According to ancient wisdom traditions, turiya is the summit of human consciousness, and attaining this state can offer profound insights into the nature of reality. Furthermore, many spiritual masters believe that turiya represents the ultimate goal of all spiritual growth. This lofty state can be challenging, but those who devote themselves wholeheartedly to their inner development can unlock their full potential and achieve true enlightenment.

Ultimately, when we achieve control over our thoughts and feelings, turiya reveals itself as a deeply transformative experience that opens us up to new dimensions of being. With time, we gradually become more connected with the world around us and more in tune with our truest selves - our souls. Thus, turiya may be seen as one's journey toward realizing one's divine nature and becoming a reflection of universal truth and beauty.

6. The Upanishads

In the Upanishads, turiya is often described as a state of pure awareness and enlightenment. As one of four transcendent states of consciousness, turiya represents the ultimate goal of meditation and spiritual practice, where we become completely detached from the physical world and delve deeper into our true nature. Some scholars liken this state to reaching nirvana or achieving moksha, while others see it as an ongoing journey that encompasses all stages of life. Regardless of how we interpret this concept, there is no doubt that turiya represents one of the holiest and most profound concepts in Hinduism. Whether we seek to embody this ideal ourselves or simply integrate its teachings into our daily lives, the power and wisdom of turiya will continue to guide us on our path to greater understanding.

7. The Bhagavad Gita

According to the Bhagavad Gita, turiya is the ultimate state of consciousness. This state is said to be characterized by perfect stillness and awareness. It transcends all mental activity, allowing us to experience a deep sense of peace and serenity. Some have described turiya as a state of pure consciousness, where we are fully immersed in inner beauty and tranquility that extends beyond our perceived reality. Others view it as a merging with the divine or spiritual essence of all things, a transcendence that allows us to reconnect with our true nature and discover lasting joy and fulfillment. Regardless of how we choose to describe it, turiya has the power to awaken us to new levels of understanding and appreciation for ourselves, others, and the world around us. Whether we are seeking peace, clarity, or greater spiritual awareness, turiya holds the key.

8. The Yoga Sutras of Patanjali

Turiya is a mystical experience of being fully aware and present in the moment, beyond the limits of thought and language. According to the Yoga Sutra, this state can be reached by practicing regular meditation, focusing on clear perception and non-attachment to thoughts or objects. Turiya can also allow practitioners to experience higher states of empathy and compassion for others and to have a greater sense of connection with everything around them. Overall, turiya represents an opportunity for growth on both an individual and a spiritual level, and it is something that anyone interested in the deeper aspects of yoga should aspire to achieve.

9. Other Hindu Texts

Other Hindu texts also make mention of turiya, though it is often referred to by other names such as samadhi or nirvana. In the Mahabharata, for example, turiya is said to be in a state of complete detachment from the material world and complete absorption in the divine. The Ramayana illustrates Turiya as a state of absolute contentment, where an individual is free from worldly attachments and desires, and their soul has transcended the cycle of reincarnation. These texts illustrate the many different ways it can be understood, but they all point to the same ultimate goal: a state of complete and total liberation from the limitations of our physical reality.

Accounts of Gurus and Experienced Practitioners Who've Accessed Turiya

Accounts of gurus and experienced practitioners who have accessed the state known as turiya are some of the world's most fascinating and inspiring pieces of literature. These accounts tell of a state that transcends ordinary awareness and pushes one's consciousness to new heights. What is most remarkable about these accounts is not just what they describe but also how they describe it: with such vividness, precision, and detail that one can almost feel their experiences for themselves.

Many of these first-hand accounts focus on the sensation and experience of heightened awareness. Some describe a sense of unity with existence, filled with lightness, profound joy, boundlessness, and grace. Others speak of moments during which time seems to slow down or stop altogether and have an enhanced perception of reality. And still, others talk about experiencing higher levels of creativity, inspiration, and intuition beyond anything they had previously thought possible.

Whatever the specific nature or qualities they may have experienced while in this state, all these accounts paint a picture of turiya as being truly awe-inspiring and transformative. Whether people find themselves grappling with deep existential questions about life and death or simply marveling at the boundless beauty of the universe, what they learn while in this state invariably changes them forever. Through their words and experiences, we can begin to glimpse just how vast our inner worlds can be – if only we know where to look.

1. Ramana Maharshi

An influential Indian philosopher and mystical teacher, Ramana Maharshi, famously described his own experience of accessing the turiya in one of his writings. In his account, he explains that after experiencing a profound sense of inner stillness, he was suddenly awakened to the fact that he existed on a much more fundamental level than he had previously believed. At the core of his being, all thoughts, emotions, and desires seemed to dissolve into nothingness. Through this transformative encounter with the turiya, Ramana came to fully understand the underlying unity between himself and all beings in the universe. Whether or not we have had similar experiences ourselves, his story offers us an intriguing glimpse into this elusive dimension of consciousness.

2. Nisargadatta Maharaj

Nisargadatta Maharaj was one of the most influential spiritual teachers of his time, known for his profound insights into the nature of consciousness and reality. Although Maharaj was highly respected by his followers, he attributed his globally renowned awakening to a process that was quite straightforward. According to his account, it all began when he had an epiphany one evening while sitting under the stars. He suddenly realized that he was no different from those twinkling lights in the sky since everything – even himself – is ultimately an expression of the same underlying consciousness. Knowing this truth at an intuitive level allowed him to access something far greater than ourselves, which he referred to as turiya – or pure awareness without thoughts or feelings. Although many were initially skeptical of Maharaj's claims, over time, more and more people came to recognize the validity and wisdom behind his teachings on self-realization.

3. Swami Vivekananda

For centuries, philosophers and spiritual teachers have sought to explain the mysteries of the human mind. While some believed that the ultimate state of being could only be reached through meditation or intense intellectual study, Swami Vivekananda believed that it was possible to achieve this advanced state by engaging in certain physical practices. The fourth state of consciousness, turiya, can be accessed by anyone who learns to still their mind and body. By following his unique instructions for physically connecting with one's inner being, Vivekananda claimed that anyone could unlock their full potential and access turiya.

Through experiencing this exalted state for themselves, individuals would gain unparalleled insights into the nature of reality itself. In this rapidly evolving world, we are constantly challenged to push ourselves impossibly further and reach new heights. Many people today credit the teachings of Swami Vivekananda with providing them with the tools they need to navigate this ever-changing landscape, unlocking their true potential and discovering direct knowledge of reality. Through his transformative wisdom, Vivekananda offers us a unique perspective on the human experience, encouraging us to find meaning within ourselves instead of chasing after external validation.

The Stages of Turiya

Throughout the ancient texts of yoga and Hindu philosophy, we find references to a distinct state of consciousness known as turiya. The word turiya is derived from two Sanskrit words meaning "fourth" and "state." This refers to the fact that this state is the fourth or highest level of consciousness. There are several specific stages or phases associated with Turiya avastha, including Sahaja avastha (the natural or innate state), kevala avastha (the absolute state), and turyatita avastha (the fifth, or highest, phase). While it is clear that each stage represents a deepening awareness and a further opening of our consciousness to higher levels of reality, there is still much unknown about this mysterious, transformative state. Nonetheless, anyone who wishes to explore their potential for spiritual awakening would do well to begin by looking within themselves for the true experience of turiya.

Sahaja Avastha: The Natural State

In the sahaja avastha or natural state, we access our highest level of consciousness without any effort or training. This is the state of true self-realization, in which we spontaneously awaken to our divine nature and experience a deep sense of peace and bliss. This state is also called "the constant state" because it is our natural default setting. We all have the potential to live in this state permanently, but we often get caught up in the noise and clutter of our minds, which obscures our true nature and prevents us from accessing the peace and bliss that is possible.

Kevala Avastha: The Absolute State

The kevala avastha, or absolute state, is one of pure consciousness, free from all conceptual limitations. In this state, we are no longer identified with our thoughts, emotions, or physical bodies. We are simply aware of being and experience a deep sense of peace and unity with all creation. This state is also known as "the witness state" because we observe the play of creation without getting caught up in it. We remain centered in our true nature, regardless of what is happening around us.

Turyatita Avastha: The Highest State

The turyatita avastha, or highest state, is a state of complete transcendence. This is when we are no longer aware of even our existence. We are one with the absolute and experience a deep sense of peace and bliss. This state is also known as "the state beyond turiya" because it is beyond all conceptual limitations. In this state, we are no longer bound by time or space, and we experience a deep sense of unity with all of creation.

Turiya, or "the fourth state," is a concept that is deeply embedded in many Hindu traditions. While different denominations and lineages describe this state of consciousness differently, they all agree that it is the highest possible state of being. Some believe Turiya is a transcendent reality beyond time and space, while others view it as an underlying state of awareness that permeates waking and dreaming experiences.

Experts who have accessed this state of pure consciousness describe it as a state of complete peace and bliss. In this state, we are no longer identified with our thoughts, emotions, or physical bodies. We are simply aware of being and experience a deep sense of unity with all creation. While turiya is the highest state of consciousness, it is also the most difficult to access. It requires a great deal of spiritual training and practice to achieve.

There are several stages or phases associated with turiya avastha, including sahaja avastha (the natural or innate state), kevala avastha (the absolute state), and turyatita avastha (the highest state). Each stage represents a deepening of awareness and a further opening of our consciousness to higher levels of reality. Learning about and experiencing these stages can help us to understand our potential for spiritual growth and awakening.

While the concept of turiya may be difficult to grasp, we all have the potential to experience this state of pure consciousness. It is our birthright. With practice and dedication, we can all access the peace and bliss of turiya avastha.

Chapter 2: Hindu Philosophy Basics

Hindu philosophy is a complex and multifaceted subject encompassing several different schools of thought and beliefs. Depending on one's perspective, Hindu philosophy can be seen as an endless tapestry of ideas and concepts or as a deeply interconnected system of traditional wisdom. Some common themes central to much Hindu thought include the importance of karma, the goal of liberation from worldly suffering, the belief in reincarnation, and the idea that all living things are intrinsically connected through a universal consciousness.

Hindu philosophy is a complex and multifaceted subject, encompassing several different schools of thought and beliefs.

https://www.pexels.com/photo/person-holding-an-elephant-figurine-7685576/

Regardless of one's particular interpretation of these concepts, they form the core of the rich tradition that is Hindu philosophy. Ultimately, it is up to each person to take what resonates with them from this fascinating topic and incorporate it into their understanding of the world. In this chapter, we will explore some key ideas and schools of thought within Hindu philosophy to better understand this complex and ancient system of thought.

The Nature of the Soul

According to the Hindu philosophy of Advaita Vedanta, the soul is a fundamental, unchanging part of all living beings. This idea is grounded in the belief that all matter is interconnected, with each individual being deeply connected to the world around them. In this view, our souls are not separate from nature but rather an integral part of it. In this view, our souls are not separate from nature but rather an integral part of it. This concept is often called "the unity of all things." Given these central tenets of Hindu thought, it is clear that one's soul is seen as something intimately connected to and reflective of the natural world as a whole. At its essence, the nature of the soul, as conceived by Hindu philosophy, is defined by harmony and unity with all life.

Consciousness

Consciousness is one of the fundamental principles central to the Hindu philosophy of Vedanta. According to this philosophy, consciousness is not only what allows us to experience the world around us, but it is also what gives rise to all aspects of our reality and existence. In other words, consciousness is considered the root of our outer and inner worlds and guides our thoughts, feelings, and actions.

Hindu philosophers believe that consciousness can take on many different forms or layers. For example, there is a deep sentient level of consciousness that permeates every aspect of reality, and there are also minute vessels or particles that carry this universal consciousness throughout the universe. While we may tend to think about consciousness in terms of human minds or individual awareness, these Hindus believe that it envelops all things in both an infinite and finite sense. Therefore, according to Hinduism, understanding this concept is key for anyone wishing to fully grasp the nature of reality.

The World

According to Hindu philosophy, the world is a veil of illusion that obscures our true selves from view. From this perspective, everything in the universe – from our most cherished relationships to the foods we eat and our possessions – is merely a temporary manifestation of an underlying eternal reality. This idea plays out in many different ways in Hindu thought, but perhaps one of its most powerful concepts is the emphasis on harmonious coexistence between humans and nature. Indeed, Hindu scriptures view the earth as a living being filled with divine energy, or prana, and argue that all people must respect and nurture this energy if they want to sustain life on this planet.

Whether we are looking at ancient Hindu teachings or modern-day practices such as organic farming and renewable energy, it's clear this worldview has profoundly impacted how Hindus view their relationship with the natural world. At its heart, then, Hindu philosophy is not just a system of spiritual beliefs; it is also an environmental ethic that calls us all to cherish and protect our beautiful planet.

Prana

Prana, or life energy, is an essential concept in Hindu philosophy. According to ancient teachings, prana is one of the primary elements of the universe, providing the vital force that allows all living things to grow and thrive. In humans, prana flows through the breath and circulates throughout the body via a complex network of energy channels called nadis. Followers believe that regulating the flow of prana through these channels can have far-reaching benefits for both physical and mental health.

Practicing breathing and meditation techniques is believed to increase the amount of prana in their bodies and improve their overall sense of well-being. So, while prana may be a difficult concept to fully understand from an academic perspective, it is a key part of traditional Hindu thought and a crucial part of spiritual practice.

The Chakras

According to ancient Hindu philosophy, seven major energy centers are called chakras. Located throughout the body, these chakras represent different aspects of our being, from physical and mental makeup to spiritual outlook. Each chakra holds different colored energy that radiates outward through channels known as nadis. Through practices like yoga and meditation, we can learn to harness this energy to achieve harmony and balance in our lives. Whether you seek greater strength and vitality or a deeper sense of connection with the universe, paying close attention to the state of your chakras may help you on your journey. Here's a list of the seven chakras and their associated meanings:

The Root Chakra (Muladhara): Located at the base of the spine, this chakra is associated with our most basic survival instincts. It governs our sense of safety and security and helps us feel grounded and connected to the earth.

The Sacral Chakra (Swadhisthana): This chakra is located just below the navel and is associated with the element of water. It governs our emotions and is responsible for our creativity and sexual energy.

The Solar Plexus Chakra (Manipura): This chakra is located in the solar plexus area, just below the sternum. It is associated with the element of fire and governs our sense of personal power and self-esteem.

The Heart Chakra (Anahata): The Anahata chakra, which roughly translates to "unhurt" or "undamaged," is located in the center of the chest. It's often symbolized by the air element due to its representation of intellectual capacity and spirituality. It governs our ability to love and be loved and is responsible for our sense of compassion and empathy.

The Throat Chakra (Vishuddha): This chakra is located in the throat area and is associated with the element of ether. It governs our ability to communicate and is responsible for our sense of truthfulness and integrity.

The Third Eye Chakra (Ajna): This chakra is located between the eyebrows and is associated with the element of mind. It governs our ability to see clearly and is responsible for our intuition and imagination.

The Crown Chakra (Sahasrara): The crown chakra, located at the top of the head, is associated with spiritual energy. It governs our connection to the divine and is responsible for our sense of enlightenment and spiritual wisdom.

By working with the chakras, we can learn to cultivate greater health, happiness, and harmony in our lives. Through practices like yoga and meditation, we can understand the role these energy centers play in our overall well-being.

Atman

Atman, or "self," is a fundamental concept in Hindu philosophy that refers to the essence of an individual. In Hindu belief, Atman unites all living beings, and it exists regardless of one's outward appearance or circumstances. While each person's Atman may be unique and individual, it is also interconnected with the larger universe. According to Hindu teachings, the ultimate goal in life is to realize our true nature as Atman and unite with the divine consciousness of Brahman. Through meditation, devotion, and wisdom, we can tap into the limitless potential of our souls and find lasting happiness and fulfillment. Whether we fully understand its meaning or not, Atman remains a central concept in Hindu thought that serves as a source of inspiration for us all.

Brahman

The concept of Brahman is at the heart of Hindu philosophy and spirituality. This is a highly abstract notion, so it can be difficult to fully understand its significance and meaning. However, at its core, Brahman is understood to represent the soul or essence of the universe. It is seen as the source of all creation and is often described as a vast, unlimited creative energy. By cultivating an awareness of this energy within ourselves, we can better understand our place in the cosmos and come closer to attaining spiritual enlightenment. So, for many Hindus, Brahman represents an ultimate truth about existence and an essential guiding principle for living a meaningful life.

Karma

According to the ancient Hindu philosophy of karma, all our actions are governed by a universal cycle of cause and effect. Whether we are aware of it or not, every time we make a decision, take action, or speak a word, we contribute to this worldview and, in turn, shape our destiny. While some may view karma simply as a system of rewards and punishments for our actions, others see it as a tool for spiritual growth and self-discovery. Regardless of how one interprets this complex philosophy, the principle of karma is deeply meaningful for many Hindus and continues to influence their lives and culture today. Essentially, it is a reminder that our choices have far-reaching consequences for us and those around us. And ultimately, our interactions with the world shape who we become.

Moksha

Moksha, or spiritual liberation, is another tenet central to Hindu philosophy. According to this ancient belief system, achieving moksha requires detachment from worldly things and reaching a state of union with Brahman, the divine essence that permeates all creation. This process can involve various stages or levels of enlightenment, including jnana yoga, the path of wisdom; karma yoga, the path of action; and bhakti yoga, the path of devotion. Ultimately, however, moksha is less about a specific set of practices or beliefs and more about a state of absolute freedom and transcendence from suffering. So whether you are looking for inner peace, emotional equanimity, or spiritual awakening, the core idea behind Moksha offers an excellent guiding principle on your journey towards higher consciousness.

Samsara

In Hindu philosophy, samsara is often described as a cyclical pattern of birth, death, and rebirth. According to this widely-accepted worldview, our current lives are just one stage in a constantly moving cycle of existence. To free ourselves from this endless spiral and achieve true liberation, we must first understand the nature of samsara and what it takes to escape it. This can be accomplished through diligent spiritual practice and devotion to the divine truth. Ultimately, Hindu teachings hold that samsara represents an illusion that can be overcome with wisdom and spiritual insight. Only by embracing this liberating truth can we transcend the endless cycle once and for all

Yoga

Yoga is a practice that has been integral to Hindu philosophy for thousands of years. For ancient Hindus, yoga was not simply a series of exercises and meditations aimed at achieving physical or mental breakthroughs. Rather, it was seen as a spiritual path with transformative powers, guiding practitioners toward developing closer connections with the natural world and their fellow humans.

Today, modern yoga continues to be influenced by these timeless teachings, focusing on quieter movements and deeper breathing as ways to tap into hidden parts of the self. Whether you are hoping to achieve physical flexibility or are simply searching for a way to enhance your meditation routine, yoga offers abundant benefits to help you reconnect with your innermost being. So what are you waiting for? Step onto your mat and start exploring this ancient spiritual practice today!

The Three Gunas

According to ancient Hindu philosophy, three basic "gunas," or personality characteristics, govern all living creatures. The first is sattva, meaning "purity" or "goodness." Individuals with a predominantly sattvic nature tend to be calm, centered, and compassionate. The second is rajas, which means "passion" or "aggression." Those with a strong rajasic quality are dynamic and driven, always looking for new challenges to conquer.

Finally, there is tamas, which can be thought of as the slothful guna. Individuals who display this quality tend to be lazy and resistant to change; they also often struggle with depression and despair. While no one individual will embody only one of these gunas, most people do have an innate leaning towards one or more of these personalities. Understanding the different gunas can help us better understand ourselves and others around us.

The Four Noble Truths

The Four Noble Truths are an essential concept in Hindu philosophy. According to these Truths, life is characterized by suffering and dissatisfaction, and the root cause of this dissatisfaction is desire. To achieve liberation from this struggle, we must first recognize the true nature of our desires and understand that these wants will never fully satisfy us. Once we have achieved this understanding, we can move on to the second Noble Truth: that the way to eliminate our desires is through a process of self-discipline and meditation. Finally, through practice and discipline, we can begin to overcome negative emotions such as anger or jealousy, ultimately freeing ourselves from suffering and reaching a state of true enlightenment.

The third and fourth Noble Truths offer a roadmap for reaching this goal, offering practical advice to help us on our journey toward liberation. These Truths are a pivotal part of Hindu philosophy and offer valuable insights into the human condition. Whether familiar with Hindu philosophy or not, these Noble Truths provide a crucial framework for living a better life. If you struggle to find satisfaction in your life, consider exploring the Four Noble Truths further. They just might hold the key to true happiness.

The Eightfold Path

An Eightfold Path is another powerful tool for spiritual growth and enlightenment. This path consists of eight different practices or attitudes, each of which is essential in achieving higher levels of consciousness. These include the right view, right aspiration, right speech, right conduct, right livelihood, right effort, right mindfulness, and finally, right concentration. By committing to these aspects of the Eightfold Path, one can cultivate greater wisdom and awareness both in your own life and in your interactions with others. One can find true happiness and fulfillment by embracing the holistic approach offered by this path and striving for continued self-development and transformation.

The Interconnection of All Things

In Hindu philosophy, everything in the universe is considered to be interconnected at a fundamental level. This idea is reflected in the concept of karma, which holds that every action has consequences that play out on both a personal and cosmic scale. The interconnectedness of all things also extends to our physical environment, as nearly every living thing on Earth relies on natural resources that must be continually replenished by birth, growth, and death cycles.

In this way, humanity is responsible for caring for and safeguarding the natural world around us for the sake of our karmic well-being and for generations to come. So whether you're a devoted yogi or simply someone who appreciates the wonders of nature, it's clear that grounding yourself in an understanding of interconnection can help you appreciate your place in the vast web of life. After all, what we do now really does matter.

Dharma

Dharma, or dharma according to the Hindu philosophy, is another central element in the religion and culture of India. While it has several different meanings depending on the context, Dharma is generally understood as a set of moral principles or duties that guide individuals and society. For example, one of the most basic concepts of dharma is Rita, or the right way to live according to the laws of nature. This includes performing honest work, caring for those in need, and living in harmony with all living things. Dharma also shapes social interactions among individuals, which includes respecting elders and holding family members accountable for their actions. At a more metaphysical level, dharma is also understood as the underlying principle of cosmic order and justice. In this sense, it represents the universe's natural balance and energy flow.

Satya

In Hindu philosophy, Satya is one of the cardinal virtues. This concept, translated as truthfulness or sincerity, holds that each person's words and actions should be intrinsically good and reflect their innermost beliefs. Satya embodies an overarching goal for the religious devotee to embody goodness in everything they do, from how they treat others to how they conduct themselves in their day-to-day life.

Practicing Satya is a personal journey needing constant reflection and awareness. It requires us to be mindful in our interactions with others and introspective about our motives and goals. Though it may be difficult at times to maintain this level of integrity and honesty in our daily lives, those who can pursue this virtuous path will undoubtedly be rewarded for their efforts both on a spiritual plane and in their relationships with others. Ultimately, by striving to live by the tenets of Satya, we can truly become the authentic people we were always meant to be.

Artha

Artha refers to the pursuit of social and economic prosperity. This concept includes any activities that help us achieve wealth, power, and prestige. While many people view artha as a wholly materialistic pursuit, this perspective ignores the fact that it is intimately intertwined with an individual's mental, spiritual, and emotional well-being. After all, having money and status can help to improve our quality of life by providing security and allowing us to support our family. Artha also encourages us to be driven and goal-oriented, which helps us achieve great things in life and furthers society as a whole. In short, artha is an essential part of the human experience that should be embraced rather than shunned.

Dwaita, Adwaita, and Vishishtadwaita

Dwaita, Adwaita, and Vishishtadvaita are three major schools of thought within Hindu philosophy. Dwaita, which can be translated as dualism, posits that there is a fundamental distinction between the individual soul (atman) and the universal soul (Brahman). This view holds that the individual soul is an eternal and immortal entity, while the universal soul is an impersonal force that governs the universe. For followers of Dwaita, atman and brahman are completely separate entities, while those who follow Adwaita believe that they are ultimately identical. In contrast, adherents to Vishishtadvaita believe that atman and brahman possess some qualities in common but are by no means the same.

Though Dwaita is generally seen as the oldest school of thought within Hindu philosophy, each approach has its own rich history and traditions that continue to influence new generations of thinkers today. Perhaps most importantly, these schools all seek to answer a central question: how can we achieve moksha or liberation from suffering? While there is certainly considerable debate around this question, they all agree that spiritual knowledge is key to attaining moksha. Through their interpretations of atman and brahman, as well as through their teachings on spirituality and other aspects of life, these three schools continue to shape our understanding of Hinduism and its central beliefs.

Hindu philosophy is a complex and varied field that encompasses a wide range of beliefs and practices. At its core, however, Hinduism focuses on the individual's journey to spiritual enlightenment. This goal is achieved through various means, including the pursuit of knowledge, self-reflection, and virtuous living. Though the path to moksha, or liberation from suffering, is often difficult, those who follow it can achieve great rewards both on a spiritual and a material level. By understanding the basics of Hindu philosophy, we can gain a greater appreciation for this rich tradition and its impact on the world.

Chapter 3: Shakti and Shiva, a Divine Union

Shakti and Shiva are two well-known Hindu deities representing specific energies: Shakti (the feminine divine) and Shiva (the masculine divine.). Though often thought of and worshipped as two separate entities, they are two halves of the same whole, and their union is essential to create balance in the universe. In Hinduism, the balance of masculine and feminine energy is considered essential for both individual well-being and the health of the cosmos.

In this chapter, we will first explore Shakti – her symbolism, portrayal, and the significance of her energy. We will then do the same for Shiva before discussing the significance of their union and how it relates to our own lives. By understanding the nature of Shakti and Shiva, we can understand life's deeper mysteries.

Shakti - The Feminine Divine

Shakti - The Feminine Divine.
https://pixabay.com/es/photos/museo-rietberg-arte-de-asia-shiva-66868/

Shakti is a multifaceted concept representing the divine feminine in both Hindu and Buddhist traditions. In Hinduism, Shakti is seen as the feminine counterpart to Shiva, the overarching masculine principle of the universe. Together, these two deities embody all aspects of creation and destruction in the cosmos. However, Shakti also exists independently, distinct from Shiva as an individual goddess in her own right. Shakti is the divine feminine energy of the universe, revered in many religious and spiritual traditions worldwide.

In Buddhism, Shakti represents latent or potential energy that can be activated through spiritual practice. Whether viewed as a representation of divine power or an internal force within ourselves, Shakti is a powerful symbol of female strength and resilience. Indeed, it is no accident that women often call upon this beloved archetype when times are tough, and they need help carrying on. Whether you look to her for support or guidance, there is no doubt that Shakti embodies all that is powerful about femininity.

Symbolism

At its core, Shakti represents the creative power and transformative energy flowing through all things. She can be seen as a representation of the cycles of nature - birth, growth, decay, death, and regeneration - as well as the grounding forces such as intuition and emotion. Her sacred symbols can be found in everything from temple art to everyday household items women use.

Shakti's symbol is the yoni, a Sanskrit word meaning "womb" or "origin." The yoni is often depicted as a triangular shape, representing the creative power of the universe. It is through the yoni that all things are born, and it is also through the yoni that they will eventually return. The yoni symbolizes Shakti's creative energy, reminding us that all things are connected.

By acknowledging and honoring Shakti's presence in our lives, we can draw on her power to nurture and protect us, guiding us along our path of growth and transformation. After all, without Shakti at the helm, there would be no life or change, or growth at all. She remains one of the most significant symbols of spirituality we know today.

Portrayal

Throughout history, the powerful feminine divine has been portrayed in many different ways. In Buddhism, Shakti is sometimes portrayed as a wrathful goddess, such as the popular deity Tara. Tara is often shown with multiple arms, each holding a different weapon or tool. This represents her ability to protect and defend those who call upon her. Other times, Shakti is portrayed as a peaceful goddess, such as Kuan Yin, the popular Chinese deity of compassion. Perhaps one of the most famous depictions of this goddess is in the Devi Mahatmya, a Sanskrit text that describes her as a fierce warrior who battles demons to protect humanity.

Similarly, in Hindu art and sculpture, she is shown wielding weapons such as swords and tridents, symbolizing her strength and courage. They are a strong reminder of the power and beauty of Shakti. Through them, we are reminded that women have played an integral role in shaping our world for the better and that we should continue celebrating their strength and wisdom for generations to come. In Hindu art, Shakti is often shown holding a trident, symbolizing her power over the three aspects of reality - mind, body, and spirit.

Shakti is also often shown riding a lion, signifying her role as the supreme ruler of the animal kingdom. She is also pictured holding a lotus flower in some depictions, symbolizing her connection to the natural world. The lotus symbolizes purity and rebirth, reminding us that Shakti is always with us, even in the darkest times.

Manifestation

The energy of Shakti has many different manifestations within and around us, taking on different forms depending on where we are and what we are doing. For example, Shakti can appear as a kind, motherly figure during times of tranquility and peace, offering comfort and support to those who need it. At other times, Shakti may manifest as a fierce warrior, defending us against all odds and helping us to overcome any challenges we face.

Regardless of how she chooses to present herself, Shakti is always there within us or around us, ready at any moment to help guide us along our paths in life. Whether we realize it or not, this powerful energy is always at work, manifesting wisdom and compassion in subtle and overt ways. When we pay attention to this divine feminine energy within and around us, we open ourselves up to all of the gifts she offers.

Power and Significance

Regardless of its particular manifestation, Shakti epitomizes all that is feminine and powerful. With her boundless energy, she shapes and sustains the world, instilling in all living beings the strength and vitality necessary for survival. In this sense, she plays a vital role in both the cosmos and our lives, reminding us of our innate power and significance amidst our intense struggles.

In times of hardship, Shakti gives us the courage to persevere and the will to overcome obstacles in our path. Her energy also fills us with hope, reminding us that no matter how dark or difficult our journey may be, we always have the potential to rise and blossom into something beautiful. Shakti is the force that drives us to live and love fully; through her power, we create and manifest our reality. Shakti serves as an external reminder of our inner strength and a constant source of guidance and comfort on our path through life.

Associate Deities

Shakti is the name given to various Hindu goddesses representing different aspects of femininity and the divine feminine. While there are hundreds of different Shaktis, some of the most revered include Durga, Kali, and Parvati. Each of these goddesses embodies a specific set of qualities, ranging from unrelenting force to soft, maternal love. Together, they form a complex web of associations with Shakti as both protector and nurturer. Whether you seek guidance or solace in your journey, there is sure to be an associated deity of Shakti that can provide the support you need. So if you are searching for strength in hard times or compassion in difficult situations, look no further than the many splendors of Shakti's divine feminine power.

Shiva - The Masculine Divine

Shiva - The Masculine Divine.
https://www.pexels.com/photo/statue-of-shiva-5935661/

Often portrayed as both the divine destroyer and the divine creator, Shiva is one of the most widely worshipped deities in Hinduism. Many consider him to be the embodiment of masculinity, embodying qualities such as power, strength, and virility. His many forms include that of a fearsome warrior, a benevolent king, and even a playful child. By honoring his power and complexity, devotees seek to connect with their inner masculine energy and cultivate it in beneficial ways. Whether through meditation, prayer, or spiritual devotion, many Hindus view Shiva as an important figure to help guide them on their journey toward spiritual growth.

Symbolism

The Hindu deity Shiva is often depicted as the symbol of the masculine divine, a fierce and powerful god who wields both a trident and fire, and he is closely associated with destruction, change, and transformation. Shiva's symbolism draws on many different elements, from his various names invoking various aspects of nature to the myths surrounding him that connect him with creation and rebirth.

Perhaps most significantly, though, Shiva's archetypal masculinity links him to primal forces and energies that are central to the universe's functioning. Through his portrayal in mythology and art, Shiva represents one of the fundamental building blocks of existence. He also reminds us that all things must be allowed to change so continued growth and renewal can occur. In this sense, Shiva truly embodies the symbolic nature of the masculine divine.

Purification

In many ancient traditions, purification holds a special significance. In Hinduism, the power of purification is associated with Shiva, the supreme god and source of all creation. Shiva embodies the qualities of strength, potency, and authority that are often associated with male energy. Purification also symbolizes cleansing and rejuvenation, two concepts central to many spiritual practices.

With this in mind, it becomes clear why Shiva has long been seen as a significant figure in helping seekers and meditators understand their true nature and purpose in life. Through intense meditation on all things pure and sacred, one can come closer to truly embodying the essence of Shiva, opening oneself up to a lifetime of spiritual insight and growth. Thus, when it comes to purifying ourselves physically and spiritually, few figures carry as much weight as the mighty deity known as Shiva.

Transformation

As one of the most prominent deities in the Hindu tradition, Lord Shiva is also known for his transformative powers. Perhaps the best-known example of this is in his relationship with his consort Parvati. The masculine divine had been begging for rebirth as a child to experience unconditional love and devotion once again, and when Parvati offered to be his mother, he finally relented.

With her love and support, Shiva fully embraced his feminine side, overcoming all of his negative qualities and transcending into something purer and more beautiful than ever. Through this process, Shiva came to embody masculine and feminine principles at once, proving himself an example of perfect harmony and unity. In essence, through transforming ourselves, we can truly come in touch with our true nature – that of the sacred force of creation embodied within us all.

Power and Significance

In many ancient cultures and religions, power and significance have long been associated with the divine masculine. Among these religions is the Hindu tradition of Shaivism, which centers around the figure of Shiva as a symbol of masculine potency. For those who follow Shaivism, this powerful god symbolizes strength, power, virtue, and fertility.

Shiva is often depicted as a wild god, dancing wildly on mountaintops with serpents draped around his body. It is this raw energy that gives Shiva a powerful significance in the eyes of his followers. However, this sense of absolute power can be balanced out by his other characteristic attributes – such as compassion for his devotees and wisdom in his teachings. In this way, Shaivism offers an ideal representation of how the divine masculine can be a source both of immense power and deep wisdom. With this unique duality at its core, it's no surprise that this ancient religion continues to inspire believers today.

Energy Manifestation

Shiva, the Hindu god of destruction, is often associated with energy manifestation. This is because he brings about change through both destruction and renewal. Through his cosmic dance, for example, Shiva destroyed the world to create it anew. In addition, he is also linked with the cycles of life and death that are an essential part of any material existence. At the same time, Shiva embodies the masculine divine, representing the universal force that sustains all things. These two sides of Shiva's nature make him a powerful symbol of transformation and growth.

Whether by destroying what no longer serves us or creating new opportunities for change in our lives, we can all learn to harness some of this energy and manifest power within us. After all, change is an inevitable and integral part of any meaningful experience - both painful and joyous. And by letting ourselves embrace these changes with strength and resilience, we can unlock the latent power within us to manifest our truest desires in life.

The Divine Union

The Divine Union.
https://pixabay.com/es/photos/buda-tantra-estatura-shiva-shakti-4642497/

At the metaphysical level, Shiva and Shakti represent the divine union of male and female energy. In Hindu mythology, Shiva represents both the destructive and creative forces in the universe, while Shakti is the spiritual energy that animates life on earth. Together, they embody the perfect balance of masculine and feminine energy, essential for sustaining life. Through their intimate union, they create the dynamic cycle of creation and destruction that shapes our world.

By surrendering to this ever-changing dance of light and dark, we, too, can experience the profound peace that comes with acceptance and understanding. Whether you view them as mystical figures or symbols of inner wisdom, Shiva and Shakti remind us that every aspect of life is precious and worthy of our love and devotion. With their grace and guidance, we, too, can connect with this divine union within ourselves and embark on a journey toward liberation and fulfillment.

The Balance of Shakti and Shiva

Shakti and Shiva are intricately linked, sharing many qualities with each other. Although often viewed separately, as a pair, they form the perfect balance: while Shakti represents dynamic energy and action, Shiva represents stillness and reflection. Together, they create a harmonious equilibrium that allows the world to exist in perfect balance. And just as there can never be too much Shakti or too much Shiva, there can never be too much action or reflection – for these opposing forces together create an interconnected totality that is integral to everything that exists. So if we want to understand, protect, and appreciate the delicate balance of our world, we must first learn to value both Shakti and Shiva equally. After all, it is only by keeping them perfectly balanced that we can truly live in peace and harmony.

The Dance of Shakti and Shiva

The dance of Shakti and Shiva symbolizes the eternal union of opposites. Shiva represents transcendence and impermanence in this cosmic dance, while Shakti manifests as energy and change. Together, they embody the cyclical nature of life, constantly creating and destroying in a perpetual interplay of light and darkness. The dance itself also represents the ebb and flow of divine energy within ourselves. Just as we are buffeted by opposing forces in our day-to-day lives—struggling against setbacks even as we strive for success—we are always engaged in an inner struggle between our light and shadow selves. Ultimately, though, it is only by recognizing both sides that we can hope to achieve true balance, allowing us to tap into the infinite power projected by the Dance of Shakti and Shiva.

The Significance of Shakti and Shiva

When understanding the significance of Shakti and Shiva, perhaps the best place to start is with a basic understanding of their relationship. According to the ancient Hindu tradition, Shakti and Shiva are two halves of the same whole, perfectly matched in every way. Together they create a dynamic balance in all things and bring order to the universe. Moreover, from a more grounded perspective, Shakti and Shiva can be seen as representing two fundamental forces: energy and consciousness. Whether or not we are aware of them, these vital forces guide our thoughts, actions, and decisions daily. In this sense, Shakti and Shiva remind us that we contain both energy and consciousness within ourselves - and that through this understanding, we can find balance and greater fulfillment in our lives.

The Symbol of Shatkona

The shatkona is a powerful symbol revered by cultures worldwide for centuries. This enigmatic symbol holds a deep significance in Hindu and Buddhist traditions, representing the union of opposites in the world and on a spiritual level. Known as "the yoni of Devi," or goddess, this magical figure represents female fertility and abundance while simultaneously embodying peace and strength. Mystical in nature, the shatkona reminds us of the many paradoxes present in life and reminds us to embrace them all with open arms. Whether used in ritual or simply as a work of art, this complex symbol holds great meaning for anyone who seeks a deeper understanding of life.

The Purpose of Shakti and Shiva

Shakti and Shiva are at the heart of Hinduism, the divine forces of creation, preservation, and destruction. Shakti is often equated with the female creative energy of the universe, while Shiva is considered masculine personified. Together, these two deities symbolize the dynamic interplay between life and death principles that characterize existence. They are also responsible for maintaining a delicate balance within human nature: Shakti brings forth new life, while Shiva works to destroy it to pave the way for new beginnings. Through their union, Shakti and Shiva ultimately represent our ever-changing relationship with the cycles and seasons of life. And while they may seem paradoxical or even cruel at times, they remind us that change is at once both necessary and inevitable if we hope to grow and thrive in this world.

Shakti and Shiva are two of the most important deities in Hinduism, representing the forces of feminine and masculine energy. Shakti is often depicted as a goddess, embodying the power, dynamism, and creativity that lie at the heart of all natural things. Her counterpart, Shiva, represents stability, stillness, strength, and determination. Together, these energies act as a kind of cosmic dance – constantly changing and moving in response to each other to create balance. By understanding how these energies interact with each other and within ourselves, we can begin to glimpse the deeper mysteries of life itself. So whether you're seeking calm or creative inspiration, Shakti and Shiva can provide the tools you need to achieve your goals. With their timeless wisdom and transformative powers, they truly are two of the most important deities in the Hindu tradition.

Chapter 4: Samadhi: The Purpose of Meditation and Yoga

Have you ever achieved a state of complete absorption in something - so much so that time seems to stand still, and you are completely oblivious to your surroundings?

Yoga is a practice that encompasses every element of our being.
https://www.pexels.com/photo/silhouette-of-man-at-daytime-1051838/

Witnessing this state in others, we often label them as "in the zone" - they're completely engrossed in their actions. But this state is not unique to athletes or artists. Every one of us has experienced it at some point in our lives. This state is known as Samadhi in yoga and is considered the highest "limb" of Patanjali's "Eight Limbs of Yoga."

Yoga is not just a set of physical exercises to keep our bodies fit. It is a practice that encompasses every element of our being - physical, mental, emotional, and spiritual. The goal of yoga is to bring us into harmony with ourselves and the world around us. In this chapter, we will take a detailed look at Samadhi - what it is, its different levels, and how it can be achieved. We will also explore its relationship with Turiya and the various types of Samadhi. Finally, we will conclude with some tips and tricks that might help you on your journey to Samadhi.

Samadhi

The Sanskrit word for 'samadhi' comes from the root 'sam,' meaning to come together or concentrate. Samadhi, therefore, implies a state of complete absorption or single-pointed focus. It is a state in which the mind is completely still, and there is no sense of individual awareness. In this state, the subject and the object of meditation become one, and there is a sense of pure consciousness. When we are in a state of Samadhi, we are completely engrossed in what we are doing, and time seems to stand still. We are completely in the moment, and there is no room for any thoughts or distractions.

In Hinduism and Buddhism, Samadhi is often described as a superconscious state that is attained through meditation. Once we attain Samadhi, we see the world through the lens of our true nature - which is pure consciousness. From this state, we see things as they are, without the filters of our thoughts and emotions. This is why Samadhi is often described as a state of "no mind," where the mind is completely free from all thoughts.

The 8 Limbs of Yoga

The ancient spiritual and physical practice of yoga originated in India over 5000 years ago. The word *Yoga* comes from the Sanskrit root 'Yuj,' which means to yoke or unite. Yoga implies union - the union of the individual self with the universal self. This goal is achieved through the practice of the "Eight Limbs of Yoga," codified by the sage Patanjali in his text, the Yoga Sutras. These eight limbs guide us on our journey from the physical to the spiritual and from ignorance to enlightenment. While the first four limbs - the Yamas, Niyamas, Asanas, and

Pranayamas - are designed to purify and prepare our bodies and minds for meditation, the last four - Pratyahara, Dharana, Dhyana, and Samadhi - are the actual stages of meditation. The practice of the first four limbs leads to developing the last four.

Yama

At the outset of your yoga practice, one of the first things you'll learn is Yama, the first limb of yoga. This concept consists of five core principles or ethical restraints, each focused on helping to cultivate a more compassionate and mindful way of living. The first principle, known as ahimsa or non-violence, encourages you to treat all living beings with kindness and consideration. This might mean being more mindful about how you eat, not harming animals in any way, and choosing not to participate in activities that cause harm or suffering.

The second principle of truthfulness helps you speak only the truth while avoiding even small white lies that might be harmful. Similarly, asteya or non-stealing encourages you to respect the rights and property of others, choosing not to take anything that does not belong to you without consent. The fourth principle, brahmacharya or chastity, focuses on creating healthy boundaries around your sexual behavior, encouraging self-control and integrity in all aspects of your life.

Finally, aparigraha –or non-possessiveness - promotes a balanced approach toward material wealth and encourages you to always prioritize what is most crucial in life - relationships and good health above everything else. Together these five principles form an essential foundation for all those who wish to embark on a journey toward greater wisdom and personal fulfillment through yoga. So if you're ready for change and growth in your life today, start with Yama - it will set you on the path towards achieving your goals both physically and mentally!

Niyama

In the second limb of yoga, known as Niyama, five positive duties form the basis of our practice. The first duty, Saucha or purity, refers to both physical and mental cleanliness and covers everything from healthy eating habits and regular physical activity to regular spiritual practice and meditation. Santosha or contentment refers to a sense of serenity and acceptance that arises when we cultivate gratitude for all we have. The third duty, Tapas or austerity, occupies a special place in the practice of yoga and is often viewed as a means for purifying ourselves through adversity and challenge.

Svadhyaya or self-study refers to the cultivation of introspection, reflection on our thoughts and actions, and self-reflection as a path towards gaining wisdom about who we are at our core. Finally, Ishvara Pranidhana, or surrendering ourselves to the will of Ishvara – otherwise known as God – serves as the ultimate act of inner transformation and understanding. Whether you are new to the practice of yoga or you have been practicing for many years, embracing these principles is sure to support your continued journey toward holistic well-being.

Asana

Asana is the third limb of yoga and refers to practicing physical postures or exercises. In many ways, this limb is unique compared to the other limbs of yoga. While the first two limbs involve practices such as meditation and focused breathing, asana is much more approachable for people who are new to the world of yoga. Unlike some of the more esoteric practices involved in other aspects of yogic life, asana involves simple movements that anyone of any level or familiarity with traditional yoga techniques can practice.

Incorporating asana into your practice can have many benefits, regardless of your level. These include improved flexibility and strength, increased energy levels, and deeper levels of concentration and awareness. Furthermore, by getting your body moving regularly through these gentle poses and stretches, you can help keep your immune system healthy too. So whether you are a newcomer to yoga or a seasoned practitioner looking to expand your horizons further, asana has something for everyone!

Pranayama

When practicing yoga, one of the key elements to focus on is your breathing. This, known as pranayama, involves regulating and controlling the flow of air in your body. By consciously slowing down your inhalations and exhalations, you can reach a sense of calm and inner focus. By paying attention to even the tiniest movements of breath within your body, you can become more attuned to the present moment. This way, pranayama is considered an essential part of any yoga regimen. So if you want to deepen your yoga practice and create greater health and well-being in your life, be sure to incorporate pranayama into your routine!

Pratyahara

Pratyahara is the fifth limb of yoga, which involves withdrawing one's senses from the outside world. This can be difficult for yoga practitioners, as we are constantly bombarded by sensory input from our surroundings. The goal of pratyahara, however, is to achieve control over these external stimuli to better focus inward. Through meditation, deep breathing exercises, and mindfulness training, yogis can learn to be aware of their inner experience while tuning out things like sounds, smells, sights, and physical sensations. Pratyahara ultimately helps us tap into our deepest inner selves and connect more profoundly with the world. So if you're interested in improving your sense of calm and inner focus through yoga practice, start with pratyahara!

Dharana

When practicing yoga, one of the critical components is Dharana: the ability to focus your mind and concentrate on a single task. This may involve focusing on the sensations in your body or attempting to clear your thoughts completely. Whatever your approach, the goal of Dharana is to cultivate mental clarity so that you can use your mind more effectively in both your yoga practice and other aspects of life.

Through regular practice, you'll begin to notice that it becomes easier and more natural for you to focus on one thing at a time without getting distracted by outside stimuli. Even when faced with challenges or difficult situations, you'll be better able to maintain your calm and composure by drawing on your Dharana skills. With time and deliberate practice, Dharana can help you become a stronger and more present version of yourself. Happy practicing!

Dhyana

Dhyana, or meditation, is the seventh limb of the path to enlightenment. This essential aspect of the tradition focuses on quieting the mind and body, helping practitioners to reach a state of calmness and completeness. With regular practice of Dhyana, one can become more mindful and gain a greater sense of self-understanding and awareness. This can profoundly impact one's life as a whole, allowing for deeper relationships with others, improved mental health, and greater emotional well-being. So whether you want to increase your focus and reduce stress or make progress on your spiritual journey, Dhyana is a powerful tool that can help you achieve these goals. So take some time today to try out this ancient practice for yourself and experience its many benefits!

Samadhi

Samadhi is the eighth and final limb of yoga, a practice that has been pursued for thousands of years. This state refers to the ultimate goal of many yoga practitioners: a superconscious state of full absorption or single-minded focus. In this state, one's thoughts become completely still, and one feels completely connected to the present moment. However, reaching Samadhi is not easy; it requires years of dedication and practice. Some believe this final stage can only be reached through deep meditation or intense physical discipline. While there are many different methods for achieving Samadhi, a commitment to exploring the inner world at a very deep level remains constant between all approaches. Through this journey, we come closer to understanding our true nature and connecting with our deepest sense of self.

Turiya and Samadhi

Turiya, or the fourth state of consciousness, refers to a highly elevated spiritual awareness thought to transcend both wakefulness and dreaming. This state can be accessed through various practices, including meditation and certain inward-focused yogic techniques. Samadhi, also known as bliss consciousness or enlightenment, is closely related to Turiya in that it involves a deep sense of oneness with the universe and all its inhabitants. Together, these states represent some of the highest forms of meditation to be achieved on this plane.

Turiya and Samadhi are often used interchangeably, but they are two different states. Turiya is a state of pure consciousness beyond normal waking, dreaming, and sleeping states. It is a state of pure awareness that is always present, even amidst the chaos of everyday life. On the other hand, Samadhi is a state of complete absorption in the present moment. It is a pure consciousness, free from thoughts or emotions. In Samadhi, the ego is completely dissolved, and one experiences a sense of oneness with the universe.

And while they are not easily attainable, those who reach them typically report feelings of intense peace and clarity, along with the experience of pure love for all living things. Thus, for those seeking spiritual growth through heightened consciousness, Turiya and Samadhi are truly transformative states that can offer deep insight into the nature of reality.

Levels of Samadhi

The concept of Samadhi can be a bit confusing for beginners since there are many different levels, and each one is distinct in its way.

Savikalpa Samadhi

There is much debate over the various levels of Samadhi, a meditative state characterized by a deep sense of peace and connection with the world. While many practitioners agree that there are ultimately three distinct levels – Savikalpa Samadhi, Nirvikalpa Samadhi, and Sahaja Samadhi – they often disagree on the details. For example, some believe that Savikalpa Samadhi can be further divided into two main levels: Samprajnata Samadhi and Asamprajnata Samadhi.

Samprajnata Samadhi is defined by a profound engagement with the world through perceptions, thoughts, and emotions. In other words, people in Samprajnata Samadhi still perceive the world around them and feel strong connections to their environment. This level is also sometimes referred to as Savikalpa Samadhi or Pratyaksa Anupratyaksa.

Asamprajnata Samadhi is a much deeper meditation in which all thoughts and sensory perceptions have completely faded. Rather than being engaged with the world through our senses or our thoughts, we become one with the underlying unity of all things in this final level of Savikalpa Samadhi. Ultimately, it is difficult to say definitively where one level ends and another begins because these states of consciousness are deeply subjective experiences that can look very different from one person to another. Regardless of these distinctions, both Samprajnata Samadhi and Asamprajnata Samadhi are considered powerful tools for connecting with our innermost selves and experiencing greater peace and harmony in our lives.

Nirvikalpa Samadhi

In many schools of yoga, Nirvikalpa Samadhi is the highest level of spiritual realization, and it marks a profound change in one's understanding of the nature of reality. This state of consciousness is characterized by complete absorption and a sense of oneness with the universe. During this state, the ego dissolves completely, freeing the practitioner to experience deep inner stillness and to commune directly with the source of all being. While achieving Nirvikalpa Samadhi may seem like an elusive goal for many yogis, those who dedicate themselves to this path will find that their hard work pays off in countless ways, both on and off the mat. Whether you are seeking spiritual fulfillment or simply a deeper sense of peace and calm within yourself, unlocking the power of Nirvikalpa Samadhi can transform your life in remarkable ways.

Sahaja Samadhi

At the highest level of Samadhi, there is a state of constant awareness known as Sahaja Samadhi. In this state, one can keep their focus on the divine presence even amid daily chaos. This ability comes from a deep sense of inner peace and equanimity, which allows one to remain centered even when faced with unexpected challenges or crises. To those who have reached this final level of Samadhi, life takes on a new sense of purpose and meaning. They know that with each moment that passes, they are slowly but surely advancing along their spiritual path and growing closer to true enlightenment. Whether running errands or dealing with difficult emotions, they know that it all simply contributes to their greater journey toward divinity. Thus, every second spent in awareness is truly precious for those who have reached this transcendent state of consciousness.

How to Achieve Samadhi

To achieve samadhi, *or a state of concentrated meditation,* you must first learn to quiet your mind and control your thoughts. This can be achieved through regular mindfulness practice or other focused breathing exercises. Once you have learned to calm your mind, you can begin to focus on one particular object or idea, such as the breath or a mantra. As you continue this practice, over time, you'll eventually enter into an intuitive state of consciousness known as samadhi. This deep meditative state can be used for several different purposes, from reading insights about yourself or the world around you to connecting spiritually with the universe. So if you are looking to achieve greater mental clarity and well-being, start by focusing on cultivating samadhi in your own life. With patience and dedication, you'll achieve this fulfilling state of meditation in no time.

Here are some tips for how to achieve Samadhi:

Practice

Practicing regularly to achieve samadhi and reach a deeper level of spiritual growth is crucial. Whether you take up meditation, chanting, or some other type of mindfulness exercise, regular practice is key to experiencing the true benefits of these activities. With consistent effort and patience, you'll gradually find yourself achieving greater levels of openness, clarity, and peace. And as you continue this mindful living path, you may eventually find yourself on the threshold of enlightenment itself.

Be Patient

It is critical to be patient and diligent in getting true peace of mind. Whether we are learning a new skill, working toward a challenging goal, or simply trying to maintain a healthy lifestyle, it takes time and consistency to cultivate the qualities that will support you on your journey to Samadhi. Patience is especially important when things get challenging or don't go as planned. Rather than giving up or getting discouraged, you should hold on to your intention with compassion and trust in yourself.

By being patient with ourselves and our circumstances, we can stay focused on the bigger picture and continue moving forward with confidence in our ability to succeed. As long as we keep doing our best every day and have faith in the journey, it is only a matter of time before we reach the state of calmness and serenity that we long for. So be patient: through consistent effort over time, you can find true happiness and fulfillment.

Surrender

Surrender is the key to achieving samadhi, a state of deep peace and equanimity that happens when we are fully present and connected to our true selves. At its essence, surrender means giving up our need to control and understand everything that happens around us. Instead, it involves letting go of ego-driven attachments and simply accepting what is. In doing so, we set aside the endless quest for empty happiness and satisfaction and instead open ourselves up to the experience of being fully alive. Over time, this deeper connection with our true selves allows us to live each moment from a place of profound stillness and acceptance, even amid intense challenges or difficulties. By surrendering to our experience with an open heart, we can gradually attain the liberating state of samadhi.

Detach

To achieve samadhi, or the state of deep meditation and connection with the universe, it is essential to learn how to detach from your thoughts and emotions. This is not an easy thing to do, especially if you are someone who tends to dwell too much on your problems and worries. However, learning how to detach gently from your experiences can help you cultivate a sense of calm that will help you to enter deep states of meditation more easily.

One effective way to begin detaching from your thoughts is simply by acknowledging them for what they are: fleeting mental events. As soon as a negative thought or emotion arises, take a step back from it. In other words, make yourself the silent observer of the thought or feeling rather than allowing yourself to fully engage with it. By taking this kind of detached approach toward your struggles, you'll gradually find it easier and easier to clear your mind and focus on connecting with the present moment. With practice, you may find that samadhi becomes almost effortless.

Witness

To reach the deepest state of relaxation and calmness, you need to first become a witness to your thoughts and sensations. This is often referred to as samadhi or enlightenment, and it can take a lot of time and effort to get to this level of awareness. However, with practice and dedication, it is possible to train your mind to enter this state at will.

Mindfulness meditation is a useful technique for developing awareness, where you simply allow your mind to be still and observe the thoughts that pass through without attaching meaning or judgment. This requires tremendous focus but can help you cultivate the mental clarity necessary for reaching samadhi. Additionally, you can also incorporate breathwork into your practice by focusing intently on every inhale and exhale. Paying close attention to how you breathe can create a sense of detachment from your thoughts and physical sensations, opening the door to a deeper level of consciousness.

With diligent work and an open mind, anyone can attain the state of samadhi and enjoy all the benefits that come with it. Whether you're looking for increased focus, reduced stress levels, or greater peace of mind, following these tips will help guide you down the path toward enlightenment.

Samadhi is a state of complete absorption in the present moment. It is a state of pure consciousness, free from any thoughts, emotions, or sense of self. The mind is completely still and at peace. Samadhi is the highest state that one can achieve in their yoga practice. It is a state of complete union with the universe. There are different levels of samadhi, from Savikalpa samadhi, a gateway to Turiya, to Nirvikalpa samadhi, the highest state of consciousness. To achieve samadhi, detach from your thoughts and emotions and become a witness of your mind. With practice and dedication, anyone can reach this state of complete peace and bliss.

Chapter 5: Yoga Poses That Pave the Way to Turiya

Yoga, this ancient Indian exercise method, can do wonders for your physical and mental health. On the physical side, yoga can help tone muscles, increase flexibility, and improve cardiovascular fitness. And from a mental standpoint, yoga can help to reduce stress levels, boost self-confidence, and increase overall well-being.

Whether you are just starting or have been practicing for many years, there is no question that yoga is a powerful tool for attaining Turiya. In this chapter, we will discuss some of the best yoga asanas or poses that can help you to reach this level of consciousness. We will also provide step-by-step instructions on how to get into each pose. Each of these asanas should be practiced regularly and can be done in the comfort of your own home.

Many different yoga asanas or poses can be beneficial for reaching Turiya. However, not all of them are suitable for beginners. We will focus on both challenging and beginner-friendly asanas that can still be quite effective. With regular practice, you'll progress to more advanced poses.

Tadasana - Mountain Pose

Mountain Pose.
https://www.pexels.com/photo/fit-woman-doing-tadasana-exercise-6453400/

Tadasana, or mountain pose, is a foundational posture in many forms of yoga. In this simple yet powerful posture, the body is balanced upright and rooted firmly to the ground, with all parts aligned in perfect symmetry. Starting with your feet hip-width apart, ground your feet into the floor and engage your leg muscles to firm your legs and kneecaps. Allow your rib cage to relax down as you lift through your spine, reaching gently upward towards the sky. Gaze forward with a soft focus or upward towards an imaginary point on the ceiling above you. Continuing to breathe deeply and evenly throughout the practice, hold tadasana for as long as feels comfortable. Slowly exhale at the end of each session and release back into a standing neutral posture before returning to your day.

Vrikshasana - Tree Pose

Tree Pose.
https://www.pexels.com/photo/a-woman-doing-yoga-in-the-garden-4457998/

Vrikshasana, more commonly known as the tree pose, is one of the most well-known and widely practiced yoga postures. This versatile posture has a wide range of benefits, from improving balance and coordination to strengthening the body's core muscles. To practice Vrikshasana, begin by setting up your body in mountain pose, with both feet firmly rooted into the ground and the arms at your sides. Next comes stepping your left foot about a foot in front of your right, with heels directly aligned.

After that, you can bring your hands together in a prayer position or place them on top of each other directly above your head. Finally, you root down through each foot and bend your supporting leg while lifting through the standing leg, holding this pose for five breaths before repeating it on the other side. With practice and patience, you'll find yourself mastering Vrikshasana and its many rewarding benefits!

Paschimottanasana - Seated Forward Bend

Seated Forward Bend.
https://www.pexels.com/photo/woman-practicing-yoga-3822191/

Paschimottanasana is a more advanced yoga pose that requires a lot of patience and practice to master. Although the name translates to "western forward bend," this posture can be done either standing or seated, depending on your current level of flexibility. To start, begin by sitting on the ground with your legs straight out in front of you. Make sure you're sitting comfortably with your back supported by a cushion or chair.

Next, slowly fold forward at the hips, trying to bring your chest as close as possible to your thighs. As you do so, focus on keeping your back flat and lengthening through the spine. Finally, once you've reached your maximum range of motion for this pose, hold the position for 30 seconds or longer if possible. Repeat this process regularly until you've mastered the pose and can comfortably hold it for five minutes or more at a time. With persistence and dedication, anyone can gain the strength and flexibility necessary to successfully perform Paschimottanasana!

Halasana - Plow Pose

Plow Pose.

Halasana, also known as Plow Pose, is a classic yoga posture designed to stretch and strengthen the entire body. This pose primarily strengthens and stretches the core, legs, and back. When performed correctly, Halasana helps to elongate and tone the spine's natural curves while building core strength. Additionally, this pose has been shown to improve circulation and digestion while reducing stress and fatigue.

To practice Halasana, begin by lying flat on your back with your legs extended straight in front of you. Next, slowly lift your legs over your head, keeping your back flat on the ground and your knees straight. Once your legs are in line with your body, allow them to fall over towards the floor behind you, using your hands to support your lower back if necessary. Finally, once you're in the full plow position, focus on deep breathing and hold the pose for as long as possible. When you're ready to come out of the pose, slowly roll your back onto the floor and bring your legs back to their starting position. With regular practice, you'll be able to hold this pose for five minutes or more at a time!

Sarvangasana - Shoulder Stand

Shoulder Stand.
Joseph RENGER, CC BY-SA 3.0 <http://creativecommons.org/licenses/by-sa/3.0/>, via Wikimedia Commons: https://commons.wikimedia.org/wiki/File:Sarvangasana.jpg

Sarvangasana, also known as the shoulder stand, is an asana that has been practiced for millennia by yogis and yoginis alike. This pose is believed to offer a wide range of health benefits, from improved circulation and digestion to relief from stress and anxiety. To perform Sarvangasana properly, one must begin by lying flat on their back with feet close together. From there, the practitioner will then gently lift their legs into the air using their shoulders as support. Finally, they will hold this position for several breaths, paying careful attention to maintain proper alignment in the rest of their body throughout the pose. Whether you are a beginner or an advanced practitioner, Sarvangasana is sure to be a valuable addition to your yoga practice.

Setu Bandhasana - Bridge Pose

Bridge Pose.
https://www.pexels.com/photo/woman-practicing-yoga-3822650/

Setu Bandhasana, also known as Bridge Pose, is a crucial yoga pose that helps to strengthen the lower back and core. To perform this pose, you first need to lie flat on your back with your knees bent and your feet pressed into the ground. Next, you'll slowly raise your hips towards the sky until your upper body forms a straight line from head to tailbone. At this point, engaging all of your core muscles is important to maintain proper form throughout the entire pose. You can hold Bridge Pose for any desired length of time or repeat it multiple times as part of an overall yoga routine. With regular practice, Setu Bandhasana can help to improve posture and overall flexibility, making it a great way to start or end any yoga session.

Matsyasana - Fish Pose

Fish Pose.
https://www.pexels.com/photo/woman-practicing-yoga-3822585/

Matsyasana, or Fish Pose, is a powerful yoga posture that can help to open up your spine and stretch your core. This pose requires you to lie flat on your back and rest your body weight on your upper chest and head. To enter the pose, simply fold your legs towards the torso, arch your back slightly upward, and press your hands into the floor behind you for support.

Once you're in the proper position, you can start to pay attention to the sensations in your body, breathing deeply as you hold the position. With practice, this relaxing and rejuvenating posture can help to improve flexibility and strengthen core muscles, making it a great tool for improving overall health and well-being. Whether used alone or as part of a comprehensive practice, Matsyasana is an essential pose for anyone who wants to harness the power of yoga.

Uttanasana - Standing Forward Bend

Standing Forward Bend.

Uttanasana, or the standing forward bend, is a powerful yoga pose that offers a wide range of benefits. From improving posture and flexibility to relieving stress and anxiety, this simple yet effective pose can do wonders for both the body and mind. To practice Uttanasana, begin by standing with your feet hip-width apart and your hands at your sides. Next, hinge forward at the hips until you are in a flat tabletop position with your hands planted firmly on the floor in front of you. Slowly walk your hands forward until they are fully extended while keeping your hips firmly rooted to the ground. Breathe deeply as you hold this pose for several seconds or longer if desired. When ready, slowly rise back up to a standing position, feeling all of the wonderful benefits that Uttanasana has to offer.

Ardha Matsyendrasana - Half Spinal Twist

Half Spinal Twist.
Iveto, CC BY-SA 4.0 <https://creativecommons.org/licenses/by-sa/4.0>, via Wikimedia Commons: https://commons.wikimedia.org/wiki/File:Ardha-Matsyendrasana1.JPG

Ardha Matsyendrasana, or the Half Spinal Twist, is a popular yoga pose renowned for its many health benefits. This inverted pose gently stretches and opens up the spine, allowing you to release any built-up tension in your back. It also stimulates and massages the organs of the abdominal region, helping to regulate digestion. Additionally, this pose can help to improve balance and stability, making it an excellent choice for anyone looking to increase their flexibility and overall fitness level.

The procedure for performing Ardha Matsyendrasana is relatively simple. To begin, sit on the ground with your legs extended in front of you. Then, bring your right foot to rest on the ground next to your left thigh. Complete the pose by twisting your body to the right and stretching your left hand to the ground behind you. Breathe deeply and hold this pose for several seconds before repeating it on the other side. With regular practice, Ardha Matsyendrasana can help to improve your flexibility, reduce stress and anxiety, and promote overall physical and mental well-being.

Pasasana - Noose Pose

Pasasana, or the Noose Pose, is a powerful and challenging yoga posture that requires focus, strength, and flexibility. To perform this asana, you begin in a sitting position with your legs crossed and your arms outstretched over your head. Next, you bend forward from the waist and reach for one of your ankles with each hand. You then draw the feet toward yourself until the heels are close to or even touching your hips. Once you have established this position, you may hold it for several breaths before gently releasing back to a sitting position. This posture is particularly helpful for stretching and strengthening the lower body muscles. So if you are looking for a challenge in your next yoga practice, give Pasasana a try!

Dhanurasana - Bow Pose

Bow Pose.
https://www.pexels.com/photo/woman-bow-pose-3822366/

Dhanurasana, also known as the *bow pose*, is a powerful yoga posture that can provide plenty of benefits for your body and mind. This pose works to stretch and strengthen the muscles in the abdominal region, including the lower back and core muscles. It also helps to improve circulation and digestion, making it a great way to start your day or break up a longer yoga session. Additionally, this pose encourages focus, breath control, and balance while helping you to relieve stress and anxiety.

To perform dhanurasana, or *bow pose*, begin by lying flat on your stomach with your arms by your sides. Next, reach back and grab hold of your ankles with your hands. Slowly lift your chest and legs off of the ground, using your abdominal muscles to stay lifted. Breathe deeply and hold this position for several seconds or longer if desired. To release, gently lower your body back to the ground and relax. With regular practice, you'll soon be enjoying all of the benefits that Dhanurasana has to offer!

Ustrasana - Camel Pose

Camel Pose

At first glance, Ustrasana might seem like a fairly straightforward yoga pose. This posture calls for you to get down on your hands and knees, with your knees hip-width apart, and slowly arch or extend your spine upward. As you extend, you should reach back along the inside of your legs until you can clasp the outer thighs or heels if possible. Hold this position for a few breaths, then release back to starting position.

While it may seem easy at first, Ustrasana requires a great deal of balance and strength as well as flexibility in both the hips and back. To help prepare yourself for this challenging pose, start with some warm-up exercises that gently stretch and open up the hips and lower back. These will help you enter into Ustrasana with more stability and less risk of injury. With time and practice, however, this powerful posture can help you tap into your full potential and unlock new levels of strength, flexibility, and focus.

Bhujangasana - Cobra Pose

Cobra Pose.
https://www.pexels.com/photo/woman-doing-cobra-pose-6787216/

Bhujangasana, also known as the cobra pose, is one of the most popular yoga postures for both beginners and advanced practitioners. This back-bending pose helps to stretch and strengthen the major muscles in the lower back while gently mobilizing the spine. It can also improve circulation, relieve stress, and increase flexibility. To enter into Bhujangasana, start by lying down with your stomach on the ground and your legs extended straight behind you. Next, place your hands palm-down on the ground beside your shoulders. Slowly begin to lift your head and chest off the ground, using your back muscles to support you. Gaze upward and hold this position for a few breaths before releasing it back down to the starting position. With regular practice of Bhujangasana, you can reap all of its many benefits and enjoy improved overall health and well-being.

Salabhasana - Locust Pose

Salabhasana, or Locust Pose, is a powerful yoga pose used to build strength and flexibility throughout the body. To perform this pose, you first lie on your stomach with your arms at your sides and press firmly through your hands and feet. Next, raise your head, chest, and legs off of the ground while keeping your core engaged in maintaining balance. Hold this pose for a few deep breaths before returning to the starting position, taking care to fully relax muscles and joints as you come down. Overall, Salabhasana is an excellent practice for improving strength and flexibility in the back, shoulders, and abdomen muscles. Whether you are a beginner just starting or an experienced yogi looking to deepen your practice, Salabhasana has something to offer everyone!

Uttar Pradesh Asana - Upward Plank Pose

Upward Plank Pose.
https://www.pexels.com/photo/flexible-tattooed-woman-standing-in-upward-plank-pose-4793284/

The Uttar Pradesh Asana is a challenging yoga pose that requires both flexibility and strength. One of the key advantages of this pose is that it helps to build upper body strength, particularly in the shoulders, arms, and torso. To perform it, you'll start by lying flat on your stomach with your legs together and your arms extended out in front of you. You then used your hands to push yourself up into an elevated plank position with straight arms and flexed feet. From here, you'll hold the position for several seconds before gently lowering yourself back down to the ground. With regular practice, this asana can help improve overall strength and blood flow throughout the body. So if you're looking for a new challenge in your yoga practice, give the Uttar Pradesh Asana a try.

Shavasana - Corpse Pose

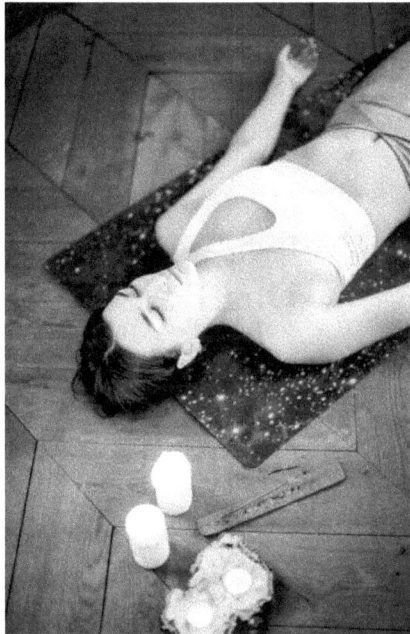

Corpse Pose.
https://www.pexels.com/photo/woman-relaxing-in-yoga-mat-3822647/

Shavasana, or the corpse pose, is one of the essential elements of any yoga practice. This restful posture involves lying flat on your back with your arms and legs spread wide, releasing all tension and stress from your body. Not only does Shavasana help to relax the physical body, but it also allows you to calm your mind and reflect on your thoughts and feelings in a more grounded way. Many yogis claim that spending just a few minutes in this pose every day helps them improve their overall well-being and reconnect with themselves on a deeper level. Seen as a way to relax and rejuvenate, Shavasana is an essential pose for anyone looking to improve their health and well-being.

Viparita Karani - Legs up the Wall Pose

Viparita Karani, or Legs Up the Wall Pose, is a simple but effective yoga pose that is great for revitalizing the body and calming the mind. This posture involves lying on the floor with your legs elevated against a wall, either straight up or at an angle. The key to this pose is keeping the spine long and flat as your legs move upward. This helps to stretch out and decompress the lower back, which makes it an excellent remedy for tightness and soreness in this area. At the same time, Viparita Karani also helps to calm and soothe the nervous system by stimulating blood circulation throughout the body. So if you're looking for a quick way to feel more energized and balanced, try practicing this simple yet powerful pose!

Adho Mukha Svanasana - Downward Facing Dog Pose

Downward Facing Dog Pose.
https://www.pexels.com/photo/woman-in-downward-dog-pose-3822118/

Adho Mukha Svanasana, commonly known as the Downward Facing Dog Pose, is one of the most popular yoga poses in practice today. This powerful pose can be challenging at first, as it requires strength, flexibility, and balance to hold it properly. However, with regular practice, this incredible posture can help to build strength and flexibility throughout your entire body while also increasing blood flow and circulation. Additionally, Adho Mukha Svanasana is great for improving posture and relieving stress, making it a must-have tool for any yoga routine.

To give the Downward Facing Dog Pose a try, start in a tabletop position on your hands and knees with your wrists under your shoulders and your knees under your hips. From here, lift your hips up and back, straightening your legs as you move into an inverted "V" position. Keep your core engaged and your breath steady as you hold the pose for several seconds. With regular practice, you'll develop the strength and flexibility needed to hold this pose for longer periods.

Bakasana - Crow Pose

Crow Pose.
https://www.pexels.com/photo/a-woman-doing-a-crow-pose-6739072/

Bakasana, also known as Crow Pose, is one of the most popular yoga poses around. This challenging balancing posture requires strength, flexibility, and focus, making it a popular go-to pose for yogis looking to challenge their bodies and mind. To enter Bakasana, start in a standing position with your feet about hip-width apart. Coming down into a low squat on your toes, shift your weight into your hands and begin to bend your arms. Then, place your knees on the back of your upper arms and slowly start to lift your hips off the ground. The key to this pose is to keep your core engaged and your breath steady as you maintain your balance. With practice, you can gradually lower yourself down onto your forearms to deepen the pose and increase the challenge. Whether you are a beginner or an experienced practitioner, Bakasana is sure to leave you feeling strong, flexible, and focused!

Virabhadrasana - Warrior Pose

Warrior Pose.
https://www.pexels.com/photo/woman-doing-warrior-pose-6787161/

Virabhadrasana, also known as Warrior Pose, is a powerful and dynamic yoga posture renowned for building strength and stamina. To perform this pose, begin in a standing position with your feet about hip-width apart. Step your left foot back and angle it out to the side so that your toes are pointing outward at a 45-degree angle. At the same time, bring your right arm up and overhead, keeping your palm facing inward toward your body. Then, lift your right knee so that your thigh is parallel to the ground and your knee is directly above your ankle. Hold this position for several deep breaths before releasing and repeating on the other side. With regular practice, you'll develop the strength and stamina needed to hold this pose for longer periods. With proper alignment, this posture can help to tone the legs and strengthen the core. Additionally, this pose promotes flexibility in the hips and upper body and increases blood flow throughout the body.

Putting It All Together

Now that we've explored the basics of yoga and some popular individual poses, it's time to put those moves together into a complete routine. Depending on your level of experience, you can start with a long flow, gradually working up to more advanced postures as you go. Some of the best, most fundamental poses to include are Downward-Facing Dog, Warrior pose, as well as Standing Forward Bend.

Whether you're focusing on strength or flexibility, these basic movements will help you build a strong foundation in your yoga practice. And with regular practice and dedication, you'll find yourself becoming stronger and more balanced – both on and off the mat. Remember, there is no one "right" way to do yoga. The key is to find what works best for you and to go at your own pace.

Yoga is a great way to improve your health and well-being. With regular practice, you can experience increased strength and flexibility, improved balance and posture, and decreased stress levels. Whether you're new to yoga or have been practicing for years, there are always new things to learn and explore on the mat. While there are many different individual poses, begin by including the most fundamental poses in your practice. With dedication and commitment, you can develop a strong foundation in yoga that will help improve your overall health and quality of life.

So there you have it! A beginner's guide to yoga, complete with illustrations and step-by-step instructions. With regular practice, you'll develop the strength, flexibility, and balance needed to progress in your yoga journey. And who knows? You might even find yourself achieving Turiya along the way.

Chapter 6: Using Pranayama to Induce Turiya

Since the dawn of time, people have been striving to find ways to improve their lives and attain a higher state of consciousness. In recent years, there has been a resurgence of interest in ancient practices such as yoga and meditation, which have numerous benefits for both the mind and body. Among the many different techniques used in yoga and meditation, pranayama (breath control) is said to be particularly effective in attaining a higher state of consciousness, known as Turiya.

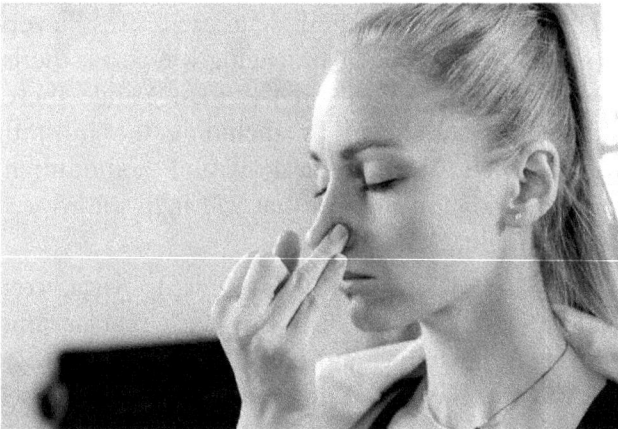

Pranayama is said to be particularly effective in attaining a higher state of consciousness, known as Turiya.
https://www.pexels.com/photo/a-woman-doing-nostril-breathing-6648567/

This chapter will explore the benefits of pranayama, both scientific and spiritual, and how it can help in attaining Turiya. We will also introduce the concept of "prana" and explore different types of pranayama techniques that can be used to achieve Turiya. By the end of this chapter, you should have a better understanding of how pranayama can help you achieve Turiya and some of the different techniques that you can use to reach this state.

Pranayama's Role in Achieving Turiya

Pranayama is an essential element of yogic practice, helping to cultivate mental and physical clarity. In Sanskrit, the word pranayama means "restriction of breath" or "control of breath," referring to the act of controlling one's breathing to achieve states of deeper awareness. Through proper control and concentration on the breath, yogis can achieve turiya, the deep meditative state that brings about a profound sense of peace and well-being.

Pranayama is also known for its therapeutic effects, helping to relieve stress and anxiety while also increasing energy levels and reducing inflammation. Whether you are new to yoga or a long-time practitioner, pranayama has much to offer in terms of cultivating greater wisdom and understanding. So why not give it a try? With regular practice, you might just find yourself enjoying all the benefits that this powerful breathing technique has to offer.

The Various Benefits of Pranayama

Pranayama is a type of meditative breathing practice that has been used in various spiritual traditions for thousands of years. This unique breathing technique has many different benefits, from helping to calm the mind and increase focus to reducing stress and promoting feelings of well-being. Pranayama can also help strengthen the respiratory system, improve blood flow to vital organs, and even boost the immune system. This ancient practice has also been shown to reduce chronic pain and improve overall physical health. Whether you are looking for an effective way to manage stress or simply want to improve your overall health, pranayama is a tool that is worth exploring.

Scientific Benefits of Pranayama

1. Pranayama and the Nervous System

Pranayama has long been used to calm and balance the nervous system. This ancient practice involves cultivating control over the breath, allowing us to develop greater awareness of our body and mind. By bringing attention to the subtle sensations associated with each inhalation and exhalation, we learn to better regulate both our breath and our internal states. And by focusing on the mental effects of pranayama, we can begin to see how the incessant chatter of our mind affects our overall well-being. Through these practices, pranayama helps us to stay grounded and present in the face of stress, anxiety, and other overwhelming emotions. Overall, this ancient technique offers a powerful way to support and heal our minds and bodies by tapping into the very foundation of who we are: our breath.

2. Pranayama and the Respiratory System

Pranayama is an essential component of many traditional approaches to respiratory health. This ancient practice works by consciously controlling one's breath, expanding and contracting the diaphragm as air moves in and out of the lungs, thereby calming and focusing the mind. Practitioners believe that this slow, rhythmic breathing regulates both the prana, or vital life force, and the nadis (or channels) that carry information throughout the body. And while the effects of this powerful breathing technique have been largely anecdotal until now, new research has revealed that pranayama can significantly impact respiratory function and overall well-being.

Studies by the National Institute of Mental Health and Neurosciences (NIMHANS) in India have shown that pranayama can help to improve airflow to the lungs, reduce bronchial congestion, and increase overall lung capacity. In addition, this traditional practice has been shown to improve blood oxygenation and help to alleviate asthma and other respiratory conditions. Controlled breathing can also improve lung capacity, regulate respiratory rate and rhythm, relieve stress and anxiety, relieve sleep apnea symptoms, improve cardiovascular function, and even reduce coughing due to smoke exposure. By harnessing the power of pranayama, we can all experience these incredible benefits for ourselves, improving our mental clarity, physical strength, and overall sense of well-being.

3. Pranayama and the Cardiovascular System

Studies by the National Institute of Mental Health and Neurosciences (NIMHANS) in India have shown that pranayama can be especially good for the cardiovascular system, improving circulation and reducing blood pressure. This is due in part to the indirect effects of yogic breathing, including lowered stress levels and increased relaxation. Additionally, pranayama itself may help to release nitric oxide into the bloodstream, which increases blood flow and helps to open up blocked arteries. Overall, pranayama is an excellent tool for keeping your heart healthy and strong, so it's worth incorporating into your daily routine.

4. Pranayama and the Digestive System

Pranayama, or controlled breathing, has many known benefits for the body and mind. Not only does it help to relieve stress and anxiety, but it can also enhance physical health, especially when it comes to the digestive system. Pranayama increases the production of digestive juices, improves digestion, and relieves constipation. Additionally, regular practice of pranayama techniques improves digestion and improve overall gut health by increasing blood circulation, stimulating healthy bacteria growth, reducing inflammation, and supporting immune function. Because of these potent effects on the digestive system, Pranayama is an essential tool for anyone looking to optimize their gut health and improve their overall well-being. So if you're dealing with a chronic gut issue or simply want to feel more energized throughout the day, incorporating pranayama into your daily routine is a great way to start. With just ten or fifteen minutes of practice per day, you can begin reaping all of the rewards that this ancient breathing technique has to offer.

5. Pranayama and the Immune System

Pranayama is a form of yoga that focuses on breathing exercises to help promote good health. One of the primary benefits of pranayama is its impact on the immune system. By stimulating certain organs and glands in the body, pranayama actively supports the immune system in its work of fighting off viruses, bacteria, and other toxins. In addition, pranayama also helps to reduce stress and anxiety, both of which have been shown to weaken our defenses against illness. Through regular practice of pranayama, it is possible to support our bodies in all aspects of wellness, from physical health to mental clarity. Ultimately, this makes pranayama one of the best ways to boost immunity and maintain overall well-being.

Spiritual Benefits of Pranayama

1. Pranayama and the Mind

By consciously controlling our breath, we can direct vital energy (or prana) throughout our body. This can have several mental and emotional benefits, including enhanced focus, reduced stress, and improved moods. This practice also promotes relaxation and inner calmness, helping us connect more deeply with the present moment. Pranayama also activates certain areas of the brain associated with meditation; in other words, it functions as a type of 'spiritual bypass,' allowing us to tap into deeper states of consciousness within ourselves. Thus, pranayama is an essential part of any well-rounded yoga or meditative practice. With regular practice, you can reap all the benefits that this gentle yet transformative breath work has to offer.

2. Pranayama and the Body

While Pranayama has traditionally been seen as a form of meditation and personal spiritual transformation, more recent research has shown that pranayama also offers numerous physical benefits. For example, studies have found that regular pranayama practice can strengthen the respiratory system, improve circulation, and help to relieve stress and anxiety. Pranayama also helps to improve focus and concentration, helping us to feel more energized and balanced throughout the day. So if you are looking for a powerful way to enhance your health and well-being, consider incorporating some pranayama into your practice today. You won't regret it!

3. Pranayama and the Spirit

Pranayama is more than just a breathing exercise; it is a powerful spiritual and physical practice with many benefits. Consciously controlling your breath can help you become more aware of your body and mind. In addition, the calming effect of deep, rhythmic breaths reduces feelings of tension and nervousness, making pranayama an excellent tool for promoting mental well-being. On a deeper level, pranayama is said to help connect you with your highest self or spirit. Through concentration and focused breathing, you can feel yourself becoming more centered, clear-minded, and calm. Overall, pranayama offers countless benefits for the body, mind, and spirit – making it one of the most powerful practices in yoga and general life.

An Introduction to the Concept of "Prana"

Prana is an ancient concept that has played an essential role in various spiritual traditions throughout history. Often referred to as the "breath of life," prana refers to the vital energy that surrounds and permeates everything in the universe. This includes living things and inanimate objects like rocks, rivers, and even entire planets.

While prana may seem somewhat intangible, it is considered a crucial part of any functioning system – from a single-celled organism to the entire cosmos. In the yogic tradition, prana is thought to be the life force that animates and sustains all living beings. It flows through the body in a network of energy channels called nadis. There are 72,000 nadis in total, with three main channels running along the spine: the Ida (left), Pingala (right), and Sushumna (central). The breath is a direct manifestation of prana, and the practice of pranayama is one of the most effective ways to harness this life-giving energy. By controlling the breath, we can control the flow of prana within the body and use it to our advantage.

Different Types of Pranayama Techniques

While the technique of pranayama may seem simple enough – after all, it is just breath control – there are many different ways to practice this art. Here are a few of the most popular pranayama techniques that you can try today:

1. Nadi Shodhana

Nadi Shodhana Pranayama, or alternate nostril breathing, is yet another popular yoga technique beneficial for the body and mind. This ancient breathing practice involves breathing in through one nostril at a time, calming the nerves and improving concentration. To begin practicing Nadi Shodhana Pranayama, start by sitting comfortably with your back straight but not rigid. You can also choose to lie down if you prefer. Close your eyes and focus on taking slow, deep breaths through your nose. Next, use your right thumb to gently close off your right nostril, then inhale slowly and deeply through your left nostril.

When you are ready to exhale, use your right ring finger to close off your left nostril while gently releasing the breath through your right nostril. Then switch the fingers you are using so that you are now closing off the left side with your right thumb and releasing the breath through your left nostril with your left ring finger. Repeat this pattern until you have finished practicing Nadi Shodhana Pranayama – 3-11 times, depending on how long you want to spend doing this exercise.

Remember to stay aware of both body and mind as you go through each step – notice any feelings of tension or anxiety beginning to fade away, and enjoy the rejuvenating sensations of calmness and clarity that invariably follow when you are done! Whether you are looking for stress relief or simply want to feel more mentally and physically balanced throughout the day, Nadi Shodhana Pranayama is a great way to achieve those goals without using complicated instructions or equipment.

2. Samaveta Pranayama

The Samaveta pranayama, or focused breathing, is a powerful breathing technique that has been used for centuries to help calm the mind, increase focus and concentration, and promote healing. To practice this technique properly, you must follow a step-by-step process that includes specific rhythmic patterns of inhalation and exhalation. Here are the basic steps for performing Samaveta pranayama:

1. Start by sitting still in a comfortable upright position with your eyes closed and your shoulders relaxed. Make sure your spine is straight, and your head is straight as well.

2. Take a few deep breaths, focusing on expanding your belly as you inhale and then gently compressing the air out of your lungs as you exhale. This will help to prepare your body for the next stage of breathwork.

3. Begin to focus on the natural flow of your breath; mentally count each inhalation and exhalation, holding it steady at five or six as you breathe slowly in through your nose and out through pursed lips. Stay in this rhythm as long as possible, working up to 10 minutes or more if desired.

4. When ready to finish the pranayama practice, slowly draw in a few last deep breaths through both nasal passages before exhaling fully out of both nostrils at once. Return gradually to normal breathing, taking note of any sensations you may feel in your body or mind during or after this exercise.

Regardless of how you feel afterward, remember that Samaveta pranayama carries many benefits when performed regularly over time!

3. Ujjayi Pranayama

Ujjayi pranayama, also known as the " victorious breath," is a great breathing technique for improving overall health and well-being. It involves long, slow breaths that are done in a specific way to maximize your body's oxygen intake. To perform ujjayi pranayama, you'll start either by sitting upright or lying down in a comfortable position. Next, focus your attention on gently relaxing any areas of tension in your body. You should then breathe slowly and deeply into your belly, using both the inhale and exhale to create a sense of balance between your body and mind. As you breathe in this manner, try to keep a gentle smile on your face and maintain total awareness of each breath. With practice, ujjayi pranayama can help you achieve peace, relaxation, and inner calm – making it an essential tool for healthy living.

4. Bhramari Pranayama

The Bhramari Pranayama technique is a powerful breathing exercise that can also be used to help calm the mind and relieve stress. To perform this practice, you simply need to take a comfortable seat, plug your ears with your thumbs, and begin to exhale slowly through your nose. As you do this, keep your mouth closed and gently vibrate your lips using the sounds "ohm" or "hum." Continue these steps for as long as you would like, taking mindful breaths throughout the process. Whether you are looking to reduce anxiety or simply find some much-needed clarity in your day-to-day life, this breathwork technique is an excellent tool that can help you achieve balance and well-being at any time.

5. Kapalabhati Pranayama

The Kapalabhati Pranayama technique is a popular breathing exercise that has been used for centuries to promote overall health. Taking just a few minutes out of your day to perform this type of breathwork can help improve your respiratory system, mental clarity, and digestion. To get started with this technique, follow these step-by-step instructions:

1. Begin in a comfortable seated position, with your spine straight but relaxed. Let your hands rest gently on your lap or your knees.

2. Inhale deeply through your nose, then exhale forcefully through your mouth while simultaneously pulling in your stomach and actively pressing out all of the air from your lungs. This movement should be smooth and controlled without any pausing between the inhale and the exhale. You should feel a light pressure pushing against your navel as you exhale.

3. After each forceful exhalation, pause briefly before taking another deep breath through the nose. At this point, you may also choose to pause at the end of each round of Kapalabhati breaths and take several normal breaths before starting again. Continue practicing until you feel calm and centered, focusing on relaxing your body with each breath cycle.

Whether you're looking to reduce stress or enhance your physical performance, the Kapalabhati Pranayama technique offers an excellent way to revitalize the mind and body through conscious breathing practices.

6. Anuloma Viloma

The Anuloma Viloma Pranayama, also known as alternate nostril breathing, is an excellent way to calm the mind, ease anxiety, and promote better sleep. This breathing exercise is simple to learn and can be done anywhere – making it a great tool to add to your self-care routine. This practice involves performing a specific sequence of steps to tap into the power of the breath and improve health and well-being. To get started with this technique, you'll need to find somewhere comfortable and quiet where you can focus on your breath. Then, follow these step-by-step instructions:

1. Begin by taking a few deep breaths, clearing your lungs, and preparing yourself for the practice ahead.

2. Inhale slowly through your nose, concentrating on drawing the breath deeply into your nostrils.

3. Hold your breath in for just a moment before exhaling slowly through your mouth, maintaining constant attention on the movement of air as it leaves your body. Try to visualize exhaling all negative emotions with each out-breath.

4. Repeat this process several times until you feel calm and centered, then continue practicing as desired to reap the many

benefits of this powerful breathing technique.

7. Bhastrika Pranayama

Bhastrika is a powerful breathing technique used for thousands of years to boost energy levels, increase circulation, and improve overall physical health. This pranayama method is fairly simple to learn but does require some practice to perfect. Start by sitting in a comfortable position with your spine straight and your shoulders relaxed. You can sit cross-legged on the floor or on a chair with both feet planted firmly on the ground. Begin by taking a few deep breaths, filling your lungs, and then slowly releasing the air.

With each inhalation, draw the breath deep into your belly and feel it expanding your lower ribs as well. Pay special attention to any areas that feel tight or restricted, gently massaging them with each breath as you inhale and exhale. Next, take a moment to close your eyes and focus all of your attention on your breath. Begin by slowly and deeply inhaling through both nostrils for about four seconds, feeling the breath fill your abdomen from bottom to top as if it were an empty balloon rapidly filling with air. Then hold this breath in for another four seconds before slowly exhaling through both nostrils for about eight seconds, emptying all of the air from both lungs at once like squeezing out the water from a wet sponge.

And finally, hold the space for four seconds before repeating this round of breaths one more time – inhaling for four seconds and exhaling for eight seconds – at a slightly quicker pace than during round one. Continue doing these rounds of deep breathing 10 times, following this pattern:

4-4-8; 4-4-8; 4-4-8; 3-3-6; 3-3-6; 3-3-6; 2-2-4; 2-2-4; 2-2 -4;

1-second inhalation/1-second exhalation/4-second pause between breaths (rounds 1 through 5); 1-second inhalation/1-second exhalation/2-second pause between breaths (rounds 6 through 10).

Once you have reached ten total rounds of Bhastrika Pranayama, take five more slow deep breaths to physically relax your body before slowly coming out of this posture. And be sure to drink plenty of water after doing Bhastrika so as not to rid yourself of too much vital energy!

---

8. Sitali Pranayama

Sitali Pranayama is a technique that involves gently inhaling in a special breathing technique known as the rolled tongue breath. To perform the technique, you'll need to first form a small tube with your tongue by rolling it along the roof of your mouth. Once you have created the proper "tube," you can slowly inhale through your mouth, drawing in as much air as you can comfortably handle. As you inhale, focus on releasing any tension or stress that may be held in your body, allowing it to flow out toward the tips of your fingers and toes.

When you are finished with the inhalation, hold your breath for a few seconds before gradually exhaling through your nose. With each repeated cycle of this technique, try to focus on relaxing further and deeper within yourself. Over time, Sitali Pranayama can help to relieve stress and anxiety, leaving you feeling calm and refreshed. If you are interested in learning more about this ancient practice and how to get started right away, keep reading further for step-by-step instructions!

Pranayama is an incredibly powerful tool that can be used to improve your physical and mental health in manways. In addition to promoting relaxation and stress relief, pranayama can also help to improve your breathing, increase your energy levels, and boost your immune system. There are plenty of pranayama techniques that you can try depending on your needs and goals, so be sure to experiment until you find the one that works best for you. Remember to start slowly and gradually increase the length and depth of your breaths as you become more comfortable with the practice. Most importantly, have fun and enjoy the journey!

Chapter 7: Meditation Techniques to Try Now

One of the most common questions people have about meditation is, what is the point? Why sit still and focus on your breath when there are so many other things you could be doing?

Meditation has been used for centuries as a way to achieve inner peace and gain a deeper understanding of the self.
https://www.pexels.com/photo/silhouette-of-man-sitting-on-grass-field-at-daytime-775417/

The answer to this question lies in the fact that meditation has been practiced for centuries by people from all walks of life. It is only in recent years that meditation has become popularized in the Western world. Meditation is an ancient practice that has its roots in many different cultures and philosophies. The goals vary depending on the tradition, but the common thread is that meditation is a way to focus and calm the mind.

There are many different ways to meditate, making it easy for you to find one you like and are comfortable doing. This chapter will explore the different types of meditation, as well as provide tips on how to make it a part of your daily life.

The Purpose of Meditation

Meditation has been used for centuries as a way to achieve inner peace and gain a deeper understanding of the self. In meditation, one gradually clears the mind of mental distractions and learns to focus instead on the present moment. Through this, we cultivate greater awareness, get insight into our thoughts and emotions, and find deeper meaning in our actions. And as we do it regularly, we can better understand who we truly are, connect more deeply with others, and experience life more fully and joyfully. These are the outcomes we want - to nourish our minds, bodies, and spirits so that we can live more meaningful, fulfilling lives.

Attaining turiya is the ultimate goal of meditation, though it takes time and effort to get there. Turiya, the fourth and highest state of consciousness, is a state of pure awareness beyond the three states of waking, dreaming, and deep sleep. When you meditate, your goal is to quiet the mind and reach a state of pure consciousness. In this state, you see things as they are, without the filters of your thoughts and emotions. You can connect with your true nature, which is pure love and peace.

Different Meditation Techniques

Many different meditation techniques can be used to achieve the state of turiya or ultimate oneness. One common approach is breath meditation, where you focus on your breath and simply observe any thoughts, emotions, or sensations that arise without trying to control or alter them in any way. Other popular techniques include awareness meditation, in which you pay close attention to every aspect of your experience as it unfolds moment by moment, and mantra meditation, where you silently repeat a word or phrase to yourself to gently redirect your train of thought when your mind starts to wander.

Whichever technique you choose, be consistent and practice regularly if you want to tap into the stillness and serenity that characterizes the state of turiya. Ultimately, what matters most is not so much the particular tools you use but rather your willingness to commit wholeheartedly to the meditative process itself. To discover for yourself what lies hidden beyond the veil of ordinary consciousness, all you need is the courage to take that first step.

20-Second Meditation

Meditation is a powerful tool that can help you stay focused, reduce stress, and gain greater insight into your innermost thoughts and feelings. One of the most effective is the 20-second meditation for Turiya. This technique involves building up to a state of deep, focused concentration over the course of 20 seconds, which then allows you to achieve a more relaxed and peaceful state during moments when you are otherwise stressed or distracted. The 20-second meditation can be done anywhere and at any time, making it a convenient and accessible way to bring more mindfulness into your day-to-day life.

To practice the 20-second meditation, find a comfortable place to sit or lie down. Close your eyes and begin focusing on your breath. Notice the sensation of the air moving in and out of your lungs. Then, start counting each inhale and exhale until you reach 20. Once you reach 20, allow your mind to become still and simply observe any thoughts or emotions that arise without judgment or attachment. With regular practice, this short 20-second meditation has the power to calm your mind and bring about lasting peace and clarity.

Aumkar Meditation

Aumkar meditation is a practice that can help you achieve the state of turiya or Cosmic Consciousness. Contemplating the sound of Aumkar can help to synchronize your mind and body with the rhythms of nature, allowing you to tap into deep levels of awareness and stillness. To get started with Aumkar meditation, begin by sitting in a comfortable position that allows your spine to be straight but not rigid. Close your eyes and take some deep, rhythmic breaths. Then, focus your attention on the sound of Aumkar as it vibrates through the air around you.

As you listen to this sound and allow it to fill your mind, try to let go of distracting thoughts and emotions that may arise. Stay present in the moment and remain focused on the experience of listening to Aumkar. Continue this practice for as long as it feels right for you, taking note of any insights or revelations that come up along the way. With regular practice, you'll be able to use Aumkar meditation as a tool for exploring deeper states of consciousness and ultimately achieving turiya – or ultimate peace and enlightenment.

Kundalini Meditation

Kundalini meditation is a powerful tool for achieving inner peace and spiritual awakening. The practice involves using focused breathing, chanting, and visualization practices to activate the body's energy centers or "chakras." In particular, the kundalini meditation technique involves directing the breath and awareness up through the body's central energy channel from the base of the spine to the highest chakra at the crown of the head.

To begin a meditation session, you'll need a comfortable sitting position with your spine straight but not rigid. Once you are settled in, you can start by taking several deep breaths through your nose and then slowly exhaling through your mouth. As you focus on each inhalation and exhalation, simply feel any sensations that arise in your body and mind. With each out-breath, repeat a phrase such as "let go" or "allow peace" until you feel ready to further engage with this meditation practice.

You can then move your attention to visualizing an imaginary line running up along your spine from your tailbone up to the crown of your head. As you picture this line, focus on activating each chakra along it by imagining them glowing bright red or gold as they come alive from inside. You can also chant short phrases like "Om Namah Shivay" or "Aum" for additional support as you move deeper into your meditative state. Continue focusing on these visualizations and sounds until you feel ready to finish up your kundalini meditation session. Then, take a few moments to gently bring yourself back into awareness of your surroundings before standing and moving slowly back into normal waking consciousness.

Transcendental Meditation

Transcendental Meditation (TM) is a unique form of meditation that has gained popularity in recent years. TM is simple and easy to learn, unlike other types of meditation, which often require intense concentration or deep introspection. To practice it, you simply follow a series of step-by-step instructions designed to guide your mind into a state of restful awareness called "Turiya."

The first step in learning TM involves identifying a mantra - a short word or phrase that helps to quiet the mind and focus your thoughts. You can either choose the mantra yourself or use one of the many mantras your teacher can give you. Once you have chosen your mantra, close your eyes and recite it quietly several times until you feel yourself letting go of any lingering distractions. Then, as you continue to repeat the mantra, you allow yourself to fall into deeper stages of restful awareness until, eventually, you reach Turiya.

That's all there is to it. With regular practice, this simple technique can help you achieve greater clarity and peace of mind, so you can experience life more fully and with greater joy. So if you're looking for an effortless yet powerful way to enhance your well-being, consider giving transcendental meditation a try today.

Zazen Meditation

Zazen, or Zen meditation, is a powerful practice that can be used to achieve inner peace and clarity. At its core, zazen involves simply sitting still and returning your awareness to the present moment. To get started with zazen meditation, first find a quiet place where you can sit undisturbed for a few minutes at least twice a day. Once you are in your meditative space, begin by taking a few deep breaths and focusing your mind on your breath as it flows in and out of your body. Once you feel more relaxed and centered, allow your awareness to expand beyond your physical senses. Continue to focus on the present moment as you allow thoughts, emotions, and sensations to arise and pass away on their own. With consistent practice, zazen meditation can help you reach a state of higher consciousness.

Mantra Meditation

Mantra meditation is a practice that can help you to achieve a higher state of consciousness. This technique involves focusing on your breath and repeating a mantra or phrase over and over again in your mind.

While this might sound simple, there are several steps to follow to get the most out of this type of meditation.

The first step is to find the right mantra or phrase for you. Usually, this involves choosing a word or combination of words that have special significance or resonate with you on a deep level. You also need to find an appropriate tone – something soothing and relaxing, but not so bland that it becomes monotonous and distracting. Once you've found your mantra, start by repeating it softly in your mind as you breathe in and out, pausing regularly between each repetition if needed.

As you continue your meditation, try to focus all your attention on the sound and sensation of your breathing. Slowly, let yourself become more absorbed in the words of your mantra. As thoughts arise in your mind, simply acknowledge them and then return gently back to the rhythm of your breathing and the soothing sound of your mantra. With regular practice, you'll begin to experience deeper levels of awareness both during and after meditation sessions, ultimately reaching the state of turiya – a state beyond thinking, where only peace remains.

Mindfulness Meditation

Mindfulness meditation is a powerful tool that can be used to cultivate inner peace and promote overall well-being. This practice involves focusing your attention on the present moment without getting caught up in negative or distracting thoughts. As such, it can help to promote increased awareness, relaxation, and clarity of mind. In particular, mindfulness meditation is often used as part of turiya, which involves expanding consciousness to the point of enlightenment.

To practice mindfulness meditation for turiya, there are several key steps that you'll need to follow. The first step is to find a quiet and comfortable space where you can sit undisturbed for at least 10 minutes. You should then clear your mind and concentrate on your breathing, observing each breath as it flows naturally in and out of your body. Engaging in some gentle stretching exercises before beginning your meditation session may also be helpful if you feel tense or tight in any area of your body.

Finally, as you start to enter a deep state of relaxation during your session, do not let yourself fall asleep or get lost in a daydream – focus solely on being present during each moment. With regular practice, mindfulness meditation for turiya can help you access higher levels of consciousness and live a more peaceful and fulfilled life.

Body Scan Meditation

Body scan meditation is a popular mindfulness practice that benefits both the mental and physical health of those who practice it regularly. To do a body scan, one first needs to cast away all distractions and focus entirely on their body. This can be done either by lying down and relaxing the entire body from head to toe or sitting upright with one's attention focused on different areas of the body in turn. Throughout this process, it is crucial to keep your mind open, calm, and focused on the present moment.

As you begin your body scan meditation, start by focusing your attention on your feet. Slowly work your way up through each part of the body—calves, thighs, hips, stomach, breast muscles and organs, arms and hands—until you reach the head and face. Take note of any sensations that arise in each area while remaining detached from any emotions they may produce. Perhaps you'll feel some tension or discomfort in certain parts of your body; at these times, remember to simply accept what you are feeling without trying to fight it. Remaining mindful throughout every step will allow you to reap all the mental and physical benefits that this type of meditation has to offer. You'll be amazed at what a difference it can make!

Loving-Kindness Meditation

Loving-kindness meditation is one of the oldest and most popular forms of meditation out there. Also known as metta or Metta Bhavana, this practice involves tuning into loved ones and sending thoughts of kindness, care, and compassion their way. To begin a loving-kindness meditation for turiya, find a comfortable and quiet place where you can focus without distractions. Once you are settled in, take a few deep breaths to center yourself and clear your mind of any stresses or distractions.

Next, focus on someone that you feel love and gratitude toward – perhaps a friend or family member who has been especially kind or supportive. When you have found your object of attention, start by visualizing yourself sending this person love and good wishes. Feel the warmth of these feelings radiating out from your heart as you focus your attention on them. With each breath, repeat an intention for the other person's well-being: may they be happy and healthy, may they be at peace, and may they experience all the joys of this life and beyond. Continue focusing on these expressions of care until they feel like second nature.

Finally, bring in some extra energy and broaden your sense of compassion to include others in your life - maybe a mentor or beloved pet - who have also brought joy into your world. As you repeat the same intentions for their happiness and well-being, try to expand that feeling outwards so that it includes everyone around you - even strangers who may be going through difficult times. With each repetition, let go of any egoistic boundaries between yourself and others until all forms of suffering melt away like fog dispersing before the sun. And when all other thoughts pass by like clouds in the distance, stay in this state of loving-kindness - pure awareness free from constraint and change at all times with no beginning or end to existence itself.

Visualization Meditation

Visualization meditation is a powerful practice that can be used to achieve deep states of relaxation and consciousness. As with any form of meditation, start slowly and develop your skill over time. If you are new to visualization meditation, here is a step-by-step guide for getting started:

1. To begin, find a comfortable place to sit or lie down, somewhere where you will not be disturbed. Close your eyes and take a few deep breaths, focusing on each inhale and exhale.

2. Once you feel calm and centered, imagine that you are standing in an open field or meadow, surrounded by tall grass and trees. Notice the fresh green colors of the plants around you, as well as the gentle sounds of birds chirping or rustling in the wind.

3. Next, imagine that there is a bright ball of light directly in front of you. This is your inner light - the source of all compassion, wisdom, and insight within you. Slowly breathe in this beautiful light until your entire being feels surrounded by its warm radiance.

4. Now that you have established your inner light as a reference point for calmness and focus, spend some time visualizing this light streaming out from every pore of your body like a fountain of energy and awareness. Let go of any thoughts or worries as they arise in your mind, instead focusing all your attention on this brilliant white flow of light within you.

With patience and sustained practice, you'll soon be able to enter even deeper states of consciousness using visualization meditation techniques like these.

Making Meditation a Way of Life

The benefits of meditation are well-documented, ranging from improved mental and emotional health to enhanced spiritual growth. Yet despite its many benefits, many people fall into the trap of trying out meditation without having a clear plan for making it a regular habit. While adding meditation to your daily routine can be challenging at first, it's possible to successfully integrate it into your lifestyle by taking small steps that build upon each other over time. For example, you might start by setting aside a few minutes each morning or evening for sitting in stillness, gradually working up to longer periods as your body and mind become accustomed to the process.

In addition, you can make your practice more effective by setting goals, breaking larger goals down into smaller milestones, and engaging with others who share similar interests. With the right mindset and approach, meditation can quickly become a powerful tool for achieving greater happiness and well-being in your life.

Meditation is a simple but powerful tool that can be used to improve your mental and emotional health, as well as your spiritual well-being. While establishing a regular meditation practice may take some time, it is well worth the effort. By taking small steps and setting goals, you can make meditation a part of your daily routine and reap all the benefits that come with it.

Chapter 8: Useful Mantras and Mudras

Mudras and mantras are two important "accessories" to the practices of meditation and yoga. Mudras are hand gestures that help to focus and enhance awareness, while mantras are chanted words or phrases that also help to calm and focus the mind. Both mudras and mantras can be used to help attain the state of Turiya or the fourth state of consciousness. In this chapter, we will take a closer look at each of these accessories, including some of the most important mudras and mantras to know.

Mudras

Mudras involve using specific hand gestures to help facilitate movement and flow in the body. While many people associate mudras with physical postures, they can also be used as tools to enhance focus and awareness during meditation. To achieve turiya, the deepest state of meditation characterized by pure consciousness, mudras can be especially powerful.

One of the best-known mudras for turiya is called Shunya mudra, which is when you cup your hands at chest height and touch your thumbs together in front of your chest. This mudra helps to build energy at the third eye chakra between your eyebrows, boosting concentration and bringing clarity of thought. Other commonly used turiya mudras include maha bandha and Ardh Chandra Bhedana, each involving different hand poses that help activates different energy centers within the body to further deepen one's meditative state.

While these techniques are not a magic bullet for achieving turiya on demand, they can be useful tools to support deeper states of consciousness during meditation practice. So if you're looking to enhance your focus and awareness while going for turiya, consider incorporating some mudras into your practice!

Kali Mudra

This mudra is said to help access the fourth state of consciousness, known as turiya. Kali Mudra has many different meanings, depending on the context in which it is used. One of the most common interpretations of Kali Mudra is that it symbolizes strength and control over one's emotions.

• Purpose

The practice of the Kali Mudra is thought to help with a wide range of different health and wellness issues. Often used in yoga, there are multiple different theories about how and why this mudra works, but there is some evidence to suggest that it gives practitioners a sense of calm, improves circulation, and offers relief from joint pain. Whether you are looking for help dealing with chronic stress or simply want to find a way to improve your overall well-being, Kali mudra is an effective tool that can be adapted to meet your unique needs.

• Symbolism

Kali Mudra is a symbolic gesture; it serves as a representation of many different concepts and ideas. Kali represents both the destructive and creative powers of nature, while the open palm symbolizes the receptivity that comes with humility and trust. Moreover, crossed fingers are said to represent surrendering to one's true self or letting go of personal attachments. With these meanings in mind, it's easy to see why Kali Mudra is such a crucial gesture for practicing yogis. Whether you're seeking spiritual awakening or simply a moment of inner peace, this simple yet powerful mudra can help you on your journey to enlightenment.

• Instructions

To perform this mudra, you extend your hand outwards and bend your middle three fingers down towards your palm, keeping the thumb and ring finger straight. To use Kali Mudra in meditation, simply hold the gesture for a few minutes while quieting your mind. This can help to calm and center you, drawing focus inward to your inner self. Some people also use Kali Mudra as a stress relief technique, taking deep breaths into their bent-down fingers to send calming energy throughout their bodies.

Whether you are looking for balance and grounding or simply seeking a moment of peace during a busy day, Kali Mudra can be an effective tool to help you achieve those goals. So, give Kali Mudra a try the next time you need a little help finding inner strength or regaining control over your emotions.

Jnana Mudra

Jnana Mudra.
https://www.pexels.com/photo/a-woman-meditating-4534592/

Jnana is a Sanskrit word that means "wisdom" or "knowledge." This mudra is believed to have a variety of benefits, including improved focus and concentration, increased energy levels, and reduced stress.

• Purpose

The precise purpose of the gesture can vary depending on which school of yoga you are referring to. For instance, in some branches of yogic practice, the jnana mudra is thought to encourage the flow of energy along specific channels within the body, leading to greater vitality and well-being. In other traditions of yoga, the gesture is seen as a way to connect with higher states of consciousness or inner wisdom. Regardless of its precise meaning or function, one thing is clear: the jnana mudra has been gaining popularity in recent years as more and more people look for ways to enhance their meditation practice.

- **Symbolism**

Jnana Mudra is a symbolic hand gesture that has been used for centuries in various spiritual traditions, including yoga, Buddhism, and Hinduism. This iconic gesture is believed to be a symbol of knowledge and wisdom and can be used as a meditative practice or simply as an element of decoration. Jnana Mudra expresses a reverence for knowledge as a key component of spiritual growth. So whether you are using this mudra as a foundational part of your meditation practice or simply as an aesthetically pleasing design element, its meaning offers food for thought whenever you see it.

- **Instructions**

To perform the pose, you simply sit cross-legged with your hands resting on your knees in a mirror image of each other. This position forms the thumb and index finger into a circle while leaving the rest of your fingers spread open wide. Some people use Jnana Mudra to balance the chakras, or energy centers, in their bodies by focusing on specific points or areas when holding the pose. Other practitioners use it as part of their meditation routines to achieve greater levels of mental clarity and calmness. Whatever your reasons for practicing Jnana Mudra, this simple yet effective stance can help you to gain greater control over your mind and body as you relax into stillness.

Surya Mudra

Surya Mudra is another popular hand gesture. Surya means "sun" in Sanskrit, and this mudra is said to represent the energy and life-giving power of the sun. This mudra has a variety of benefits, including improved focus and concentration, increased energy levels, and reduced stress. Whether you are an experienced yogi or just beginning your journey into meditation, Surya Mudra is a simple but powerful tool for promoting well-being in body and mind.

- **Purpose**

Surya Mudra is a hand gesture that is commonly used in yoga and meditation practices. The purpose of this mudra is to help stimulate the energy centers of the body, - your chakras, by applying gentle pressure to specific points on the hands. By activating these energy centers, we can promote physical and mental health, reduce stress and anxiety, and enhance clarity of mind. With regular practice of this mudra, you can reap all the many benefits that it has to offer.

- **Symbolism**

Surya Mudra, also known as the "gesture of the sun," is an ancient finger pose with a rich heritage and powerful symbolism. This mudra is thought to be naturally energizing and warming, symbolizing both the sun's light and its life-giving power. According to traditional belief, practicing Surya Mudra can help revitalize your body, increase creativity, boost immunity, and awaken positive energy. Whether you practice this mudra as part of your daily yoga routine or simply as a way to center yourself during stressful times, it holds great potential for improving your mental, physical, and spiritual well-being. So why not go ahead and try out this simple yet meaningful meditative gesture for yourself? You might just be surprised by the benefits that it has in store for you!

- **Instructions**

The Surya Mudra is a simple hand gesture that can be used to improve circulation, reduce stress, and promote feelings of calm and well-being. This mudra involves placing the tips of your thumb and index finger together, giving the rest of your hand a loose and open appearance. To perform this mudra, simply sit comfortably with your hands in your lap or at your sides. Then, gently touch the tips of your thumb and index finger together, maintaining this position for five to ten minutes at a time. Not only is the Surya Mudra an easy way to increase overall health and well-being, but it can also be practiced anywhere - no special equipment or instruction is required.

Mantras

A mantra is a word or phrase that is repeated during meditation to enhance focus and awareness. During deep meditative states, such as Turiya, mantras can be extremely effective for clearing distractions and helping to direct the mind towards stillness. Some of the most common mantras are simple repetitions of a single word, such as "peace" or "calm," while others incorporate more complex linguistic patterns that engage both the intellect and the emotions. Whatever form it takes, a mantra is a focused tool that can help to clarify one's intention and deepen their meditative experience. So whether you are just starting or you are looking to take your practice to new depths, incorporating mantras into your daily routine can be an excellent way to enhance your ability to achieve Turiya.

Om Shanti Shanti Shanti

Om Shanti, Shanti, Shanti is a sacred mantra that is used to promote inner peace and connect with the divine. This mantra can be repeated in times of stress or struggle to help soothe the mind and calm the soul. Through its peaceful vibrations, this mantra helps to align us with the universe and connect us with our higher selves.

- **Pronunciation**

Pronounced "ohm Shahn-tee Shahn-tee," this mantra is made up of three Sanskrit words that can be translated to mean "peace," "calm," and "quiet."

- **Meaning**

This simple yet profound invocation is traditionally understood as a form of meditation on divine peace. This mantra can be used as a tool to help clear the mind, focus the senses, and cultivate a sense of inner calm. In addition, many yogis believe that repeating the Om Shanti Shanti Shanti mantra can help to bring forth one's inner light or energy, supporting one's journey toward higher levels of spiritual awareness.

- **Significance**

The mantra Om Shanti Shanti Shanti has healing properties, helping us restore balance and harmony within our bodies and minds. Whether you are looking for spiritual guidance or simply searching for a little peace in your life, chanting Om Shanti Shanti Shanti can be a powerful tool for finding tranquility and enlightenment. So if you're looking to reconnect with yourself and your true purpose, let this ancient mantra help guide you home. Om Shanti, Shanti, Shanti.

Aum Namah Shivaya

Aum Namah Shivaya is a sacred mantra that is used to honor the Hindu deity, Shiva. It is often repeated during meditation as a way to connect with Shiva's energy and receive his blessings. In addition, Aum Namah Shivaya is also used as a tool for self-purification, helping us to let go of negative thoughts and emotions that may be holding us back.

- **Pronunciation**

Pronounced "ohm Nah-mah shi-vie-yah," this mantra is made up of four Sanskrit words that can be translated to mean "I bow to Shiva."

- **Meaning**

Aum Namah Shivaya is a sacred chant that is typically used as a mantra in meditation and spiritual practice. The powerful Sanskrit words are thought to help bring the individual into a deeper state of awareness, helping connect with the divine forces at work in the universe. According to tradition, Aum Namah Shivaya reflects the beginning, middle, and end of all things. It is said to embody the primordial vibration of creation and represents both struggle and release. In many ways, these two opposing forces form the core of human existence: from birth to death, we fight and strive for progress even as we inevitably succumb to decline and decay. Despite this hard truth about life, Aum Namah Shivaya reminds us that peace and contentment can be found through liberation from our earthly suffering. Through repetition of these sacred words and deep focus during meditation, we can come one step closer to finding this peace within ourselves.

- **Significance**

Aum Namah Shivaya is an ancient Sanskrit mantra that is said to be positively charged with spiritual energy. This powerful mantra has been used for centuries for enlightenment, helping people connect with the divine and release their innermost desires. But perhaps its greatest significance lies in its capacity to create feelings of peace and calm within the heart and mind. One can access a deep sense of inner tranquility by chanting this sacred phrase, allowing one to confront life's challenges with optimism and clarity. So whether you are looking for a way to connect with your spirituality or simply seeking some much-needed peace and stillness in your life, Aum Namah Shivaya is sure to offer profound insight and healing.

So Hum

The So Hum mantra is a powerful tool for connecting with your inner wisdom and tapping into the profound wisdom of the universe. This mantra consists of three simple words–so, hum, and so–which represent the balance between the self and the greater whole. By repeating this mantra and bringing your full focus to the sound of each word, you can quiet your mind, open your heart, and connect deeply with yourself as well as with all beings everywhere. In this way, the So Hum mantra is a healing and transformative practice that has been used for generations to promote peace, insight, and understanding.

- **Pronunciation**

Pronounced "soh-hum," this mantra is made up of two Sanskrit words that can be translated to mean "I am that."

- **Meaning**

The So Hum mantra is foundational in the yogic tradition. Also known as the "I am" or "The Secret Sound," this phrase is used as an affirmation of one's divinity and connects the individual with their higher self. Its meaning can also be interpreted more broadly as a reminder to stay grounded, connected with the present moment, and focused on what's truly important in life. Whether you are practicing yoga or simply trying to quiet your mind and focus your attention, the So Hum mantra can be very powerful for calming your mind and finding clarity in even the most stressful circumstances. Ultimately, this ancient Sanskrit phrase embodies the essence of transformation and spiritual awakening, reminding us that we are always exactly where we need to be.

- **Significance**

The So Hum mantra is a key element of yoga and meditation practice. Also known as the primordial rhythm, this mantra helps to bring balance and alignment to mind, body, and spirit. Focusing our attention on the So Hum sound can help us still the mind, connect more deeply with our inner self, and move toward greater harmony and well-being. Furthermore, simply reciting the mantra can profoundly affect our energy levels and emotional state. Whether you are looking to quiet your mind during meditation or increase your sense of peace and contentment in your daily life, the So Hum mantra holds great power and significance.

Mudras and mantras are two powerful tools used for self-transformation and healing. Mudras are hand gestures that help direct energy flow within the body, while mantras are sacred words or phrases that have positive spiritual effects. Both mudras and mantras can be used to promote feelings of peace, calm, and well-being. When used together, they can be incredibly powerful when used for self-care and personal growth. If you want to improve your well-being, consider incorporating mudras and mantras into your daily routine.

Chapter 9: Yoga Sequences to Unlock Turiya

Creating a daily yoga practice can greatly improve your flexibility, strength, and overall sense of well-being. However, with so many different techniques to choose from, it can be difficult to know where to start. In this chapter, we will put together all of the various poses, breathing techniques, meditation methods, mantras, and mudras into complete sequences that can be done daily or several times a day. Doing these sequences regularly will help you to create a healthy mind-body-spirit balance in your life.

Creating a daily yoga practice can be a great way to improve your flexibility, strength, and overall sense of well-being.

https://www.pexels.com/photo/low-angle-view-of-woman-relaxing-on-beach-against-blue-sky-317157/

Monday Sequence

Starting your week off with yoga practice is a great way to set the tone for the rest of your week. This sequence will help you connect with your breath, center yourself, and release any tension you may be holding onto from the weekend.

Meditation Technique: Mindfulness Meditation

Begin by sitting in a comfortable position and focusing on your breath. Notice the sensation of the air moving in and out of your nose and lungs. Don't try to control your breath; just let it flow naturally. If your mind starts to wander, gently bring your attention back to your breath.

Breathing Technique: 4-7-8 Breathing

After you have finished your mindfulness meditation, do 4-7-8 breathing to help you relax. Breathe in for a count of four, hold your breath for a count of seven, and then exhale for a count of eight. Repeat this cycle several times.

Yoga Pose: Cat-Cow Pose

Start on your hands and knees in a "tabletop" position. As you inhale, drop your belly and look up towards the ceiling, letting your spine arch. As you exhale, round your spine up towards the ceiling and tuck your chin to your chest. Repeat this pose several times, moving slowly and smoothly with your breath.

Yoga Pose: Downward-Facing Dog

From your tabletop position, tuck your toes under and lift your hips up and back, coming into an "inverted V" shape. Straighten your legs as much as you can without compromising the natural curve of your spine. Let your head hang down and relax your shoulders. Stay in this pose for at least five breaths.

Yoga Pose: Warrior II

From Downward Facing Dog, step your right foot forward between your hands. Align your right knee over your right ankle and square your hips towards the front of your mat. Reach your arms out to the sides, parallel to the ground, and look over your right hand. Hold this pose for five breaths before switching to the other side.

Mantra: So Hum

After you have finished your Warrior II pose, come back to Downward Facing Dog and take a few deep breaths. Then, sit in a comfortable position and close your eyes. Repeat the mantra "so hum" to yourself silently. This mantra can be translated to mean "I am that" or "I am everything." Allow the mantra to sink in and just be with the feeling of it.

Mudra: Gyan Mudra

Finish your Monday sequence by sitting in a comfortable position and taking a few deep breaths. Place your hands in your lap with your palms facing up. Bring your index finger and thumb together to form a circle. This mudra is known as the "mudra of knowledge" and is said to promote concentration and clarity of thought.

Tuesday Sequence

On Tuesdays, we will focus on building strength and energy. This sequence includes some standing poses that will help to improve your balance and coordination.

Yoga Pose: Mountain Pose

Stand with your feet hip-width apart and your arms by your sides. Engage your core muscles and lift your shoulders up and back. Gaze forward and take a few deep breaths.

Yoga Pose: Half Camel Pose

From Mountain Pose, place your right hand on your lower back and reach your left arm up towards the ceiling. Gently arch your back and look up towards the ceiling. Hold this pose for five breaths before switching to the other side.

Yoga Pose: Chair Pose

From Mountain Pose, bend your knees and lower your hips down into a "chair" position. Keep your knees aligned over your ankles, and try to bring your thighs parallel to the ground. Reach your arms up towards the ceiling and hold this pose for five breaths.

Meditation: Body Scan

After you have finished your Chair Pose, find a comfortable seat. Close your eyes and take a few deep breaths. Starting at your feet, focus your attention on each part of your body and notice any sensations or emotions that you are experiencing. Don't try to judge or change anything; just observe and let go.

Mantra: Aum Namah Shivaya

When you have finished your body scan, sit for a few more minutes and repeat the mantra "Aum Namah Shivaya" to yourself. This mantra is a tribute to Lord Shiva, the Hindu god of destruction. It is said to promote peace and serenity.

Mudra: Ganesha Mudra

To end your Tuesday sequence, place one hand over the other, with the upper hand resting at the level of the heart. The thumb, index finger, and middle finger should all be touching, forming a triangle shape. The ring finger should be bent and pulled back, while the pinky finger should be extended and pointed outwards. By activating the Ganesha mudra, you can tap into your inherent inner wisdom to unlock your full potential on both physical and spiritual levels.

Wednesday Sequence

On Wednesdays, we will focus on flexibility and releasing tension. This sequence includes some gentle stretches that will help to release any tightness in your muscles.

Yoga Pose: Child's Pose

From a seated position, bring your knees up towards your chest and then slowly lower your hips back down to your heels. Rest your forehead on the ground and extend your arms out in front of you. Take a few deep breaths and hold this pose for as long as you like.

Yoga Pose: Cat/Cow Pose

From Child's Pose, move into an all-fours position with your wrists aligned under your shoulders and your knees aligned under your hips. As you inhale, arch your back and look up towards the ceiling. As you exhale, round your back and tuck your chin towards your chest. Continue this flow for a few breaths.

Yoga Pose: Pigeon Pose

From Cat/Cow Pose, bring your right knee forward and place it behind your right wrist. Slowly lower your left leg back and extend your right leg out behind you. You can place a blanket under your hips for support. Hold this pose for five breaths before switching to the other side.

Meditation: Loving-Kindness

After you have finished your Pigeon Pose, find a comfortable seat. Close your eyes and take a few deep breaths. Think of someone in your life who you love and send them thoughts of warmth, compassion, and love. Then, extend those same thoughts to yourself.

Mantra: Om Mani Padme Hum

When you have finished your meditation, sit for a few more minutes and repeat the mantra "Om Mani Padme Hum" to yourself. This mantra is said to be the key to enlightenment and is used as a prayer for compassion.

Mudra: Compassion Mudra

To end your Wednesday sequence, sit in a comfortable position and place your hands in your lap with your palms facing up. Bring your thumb and middle finger together while keeping your index and ring finger extended. This mudra is known as the "mudra of compassion" and is said to promote feelings of love and understanding.

Thursday Sequence

On Thursdays, we will focus on balance and centering ourselves. This sequence includes some standing poses that will help to improve your balance and coordination.

Yoga Pose: Tree Pose

From a standing position, move your weight onto your left foot and bring your right foot up to rest on your left thigh. Keep your hips squared and your arms at your sides. Take a deep breath and raise your arms overhead. Hold this pose for five breaths before switching to the other side.

Yoga Pose: Half Moon Pose

From Tree Pose, bring your right hand down to the ground and lift your left leg. Keep your gaze focused on a fixed point in front of you to help with balance. Hold this pose for five breaths before switching to the other side.

Yoga Pose: Warrior III

From Half Moon Pose, lower your left leg back down to the ground and bring your arms back by your sides. Shift your weight onto your right foot and lift your left leg behind you. Lean forward from the hips, keeping your back straight. Hold this pose for five breaths before switching to the other side.

Meditation: Centering

After you have finished Warrior III, find a comfortable seat. Close your eyes and take a few deep breaths. Focus your attention on your breath and let all other thoughts fall away. Stay here for as long as you like.

Mantra: Om Gam Ganapataye Namah

When you have finished your meditation, sit for a few more minutes and repeat the mantra "Om Gam Ganapataye Namah" to yourself. This mantra is a prayer to Lord Ganesha, the Hindu god of wisdom and new beginnings.

Mudra: Shankh Mudra

To end your Thursday sequence, sit comfortably and place your hands in your lap with your palms facing up. Bring your thumb and index finger together while extending your middle, ring, and pinky fingers. With your right hand, form a "C" shape and place the back of your hand on top of your left, forming a conch shell. This mudra promotes calmness and stability.

Friday Sequence

On Fridays, we will focus on twists and releasing any tension that has built up during the week. This sequence includes some standing and seated Twist poses that will help to stretch and relax your muscles.

Yoga Pose: Half Camel Pose

From a standing position, kneel on your mat with your knees hip-width apart. Place your hands on your lower back and lean back, letting your head fall back as well. Hold this pose for five breaths.

Yoga Pose: Seated Twist

From Half Camel Pose, sit up and bring your legs out in front of you. Cross your right leg over your left and place your right hand on the ground behind you. Place your left hand on your right knee and twist your torso to the right. Hold this pose for five breaths before switching to the other side.

Yoga Pose: Half Lord of the Fishes Pose

From Seated Twist, bring your legs back into Half Camel Pose. Reach your left arm up overhead and then twist your torso to the right, bringing your left arm down to the ground behind you. Look over your right shoulder. Hold this pose for five breaths before switching to the other side.

Yoga Pose: Revolved Triangle Pose

From Half Lord of the Fishes Pose, straighten your legs and move into Triangle Pose. Reach your right arm up overhead and your left hand down to the ground. Twist your torso to the right, looking over your right shoulder. Hold this pose for five breaths before switching to the other side.

Meditation: Release

After you have finished Revolved Triangle Pose, find a comfortable place to sit. Close your eyes and take a few deep breaths. Focus your attention on your breath and let all other thoughts fall away. Stay here for as long as you like.

Mantra: Om Namah Shivaya

When you have finished your meditation, sit for a few more minutes and repeat the mantra "Om Namah Shivaya" to yourself. This mantra is a prayer to Lord Shiva, the Hindu god of destruction.

Mudra: Aum Mudra

To end your Friday sequence, sit with your spine straight. Bring your hands to your knees with your palms up. Bend your index and middle fingers down to touch the base of your thumb. Extend your ring and pinky fingers.

Saturday Sequence

On Saturdays, we will focus on deep stretches and relaxation. This sequence includes some restorative yoga poses that will help to stretch and relax your muscles.

Yoga Pose: Child's Pose

From a kneeling position, lower your torso down to your mat and stretch your arms out in front of you. Rest your forehead on the mat and breathe deeply. Hold this pose for five breaths.

Yoga Pose: Pigeon Pose

From Child's Pose, bring your right leg forward and place it in front of you so that your knee is next to your right wrist and your ankle is next to your left hip. Your left leg should be extended straight back behind you. Lower your torso down to the mat and rest your forehead on your mat. Hold this pose for five breaths before switching to the other side.

Yoga Pose: Sphinx Pose

From Pigeon Pose, lower your torso down to the mat and slide your left leg back so that both legs are extended straight behind you. Place your elbows under your shoulders and prop yourself up on your forearms. Hold this pose for five breaths.

Meditation: Visualize

After you have finished Sphinx Pose, lie down on your mat and close your eyes. Take a few deep breaths and begin to visualize a peaceful place. It can be somewhere you've been before or somewhere you've never been. Imagine all of the details of this place – the sights, the sounds, the smells. Stay here for as long as you like.

Mantra: Om Mani Padme Hum

When you have finished your visualization, sit up and repeat the mantra "Om Mani Padme Hum" to yourself. This mantra is a prayer to the Buddha of compassion, Chenrezig.

Mudra: Compassion Mudra

To end your Saturday sequence, sit in a comfortable position with your spine straight. Bring your hands to your heart center, with your right hand cupping your left. This mudra is known as the "mudra of compassion" and is said to promote feelings of love and kindness.

Sunday Sequence

On Sundays, we will take a break from our routine and focus on self-care. This may include taking a relaxing bath, reading your favorite book, or spending time with loved ones. Do whatever you need to do to recharge and rejuvenate yourself for the week ahead. Walking in nature, eating healthy foods, and getting enough sleep are also great ways to care for yourself.

Relaxing Bath: Add some soothing aromatherapy or add a few drops of lavender oil to your bathtub to help you relax.

Reading: Curl up with your favorite book and escape into another world for a while.

Time with Loved Ones: Spend time with family or friends, or reach out to someone you haven't talked to in a while.

Walking in Nature: Take a walk in the park or the woods and appreciate the beauty around you.

Eating Healthy Foods: Fill your body with nourishing foods that will make you feel good.

Getting Enough Sleep: Make sure you get enough sleep each night to help your body and mind rest and recharge.

These are just a few examples of the many different types of sequences you can do at home to improve your health and well-being. Remember to listen to your body and breathing, and let go of any expectations or goals you have for your practice. Just be present in the moment and enjoy the process. While it is important to challenge yourself, find what feels good for your body and do what you can to nurture your mind, body, and soul.

Chapter 10: Your Daily Steps Towards Turiya

To achieve Turiya, it is crucial to have a lifestyle that is dedicated to this goal. This means more than just meditating or doing yoga every day. It requires a change in mindset and a commitment to becoming aware of one's thoughts, emotions, and actions. While it may seem like a daunting task, making this change in perspective is essential to successfully reaching Turiya. There are many ways to begin this journey, but some key practices include self-reflection, mindfulness, and compassion. These three pillars will help to lay the foundation for a more conscious way of living that will eventually lead to Turiya.

To achieve Turiya, it is crucial to have a lifestyle that is dedicated to this goal.
https://www.pexels.com/photo/silhouette-of-person-raising-its-hand-268134/

This chapter will give you a week-long schedule you can repeat to get closer to Turiya. Other than daily recommendations of meditation and yoga sequences, various other tips and tricks will be included, such as reminders to practice mindfulness, become aware of your consciousness, and get used to "becoming a witness" in your life. By following this schedule and implementing these tips, anyone can begin to live a more conscious and fulfilling life.

The Lifestyle of Turiya

Turiya is a lifestyle of peace and mindfulness. A key piece to this lifestyle is a devotion to creating inner awareness and equilibrium in all areas of life. Whether you are working, parenting, or simply taking a moment for yourself, Turiya encourages you to always be present and aware of the moment. This holistic approach means that you can enjoy everything from mindful eating and exercise routines to creative hobbies and social engagements while embracing an attitude of acceptance, appreciation, and relaxation. By viewing your life in this way, you are better able to live with joy, purpose, and fulfillment as you savor each experience as it comes. The more balanced you are on the inside, the better you'll feel on the outside.

Tips and Tricks for Achieving Turiya

To achieve turiya, or the state of pure, transcendent consciousness, you have to step out of your normal routine and make some key changes in your daily habits.

Diet

One of the most basic things to focus on is diet. Since turiya is a meditative state where you experience deep, natural peace and harmony, your diet should be high in nutrients that promote healthy mental functioning. This may mean cutting back on caffeine and foods that are high in sugar, both of which can have a counterproductive effect on the clarity of the mind.

Meditation and Yoga

No discussion of turiya would be complete without mentioning the importance of meditation and yoga. These two practices go hand-in-hand to achieve a deeper level of consciousness. Meditation helps to still the mind and bring about inner peace, while yoga helps to physically align the body and create balance in the mind-body connection. The goal is to reach a state of complete harmony between the two.

Mindfulness

Mindfulness is key to achieving turiya. It means being present in the moment and being aware of your thoughts, emotions, and actions. It may seem difficult at first, but with practice, it will become second nature. One way to be more mindful is to focus on your breath and use it as an anchor to bring you back to the present moment whenever your mind wanders.

Compassion

Having compassion is an essential ingredient in the recipe for turiya. This doesn't mean that you have to be a doormat or agree with everything everyone says, but it does mean that you should try to see things from other people's perspectives and always be respectful. By cultivating compassion, you'll be able to find common ground with others and build strong, lasting relationships.

Awareness

Paying attention is also necessary to reach a higher state of mindfulness. Be aware of your thoughts, emotions, and actions, as well as the thoughts, emotions, and actions of others. It may seem like a challenge at first, but with practice, it will become easier . . . and soon, second nature. The more aware you are, the better able you'll be to find balance in your life and live with purpose and fulfillment.

Becoming a Witness

One of the best things you can do to achieve turiya is to become a witness to your own life. This means watching your thoughts and emotions without judgment or attachment. It may sound easy, but in reality, it's quite difficult. The key is to practice detachment and focus on the present moment. By doing this, you'll see things more clearly and find balance in your life.

Acceptance

Last but not least, it's essential to accept yourself and others. This means accepting your thoughts, emotions, and actions as well as the thoughts, emotions, and actions of others. It may seem difficult at first, but with practice, it will become easier. The more you accept yourself and others, the more balanced you'll be in your life and the closer you'll be to achieving turiya.

Practice Self-Reflection

One of the best ways to achieve turiya is to practice self-reflection. This is all about taking some time each day to sit quietly and reflect on your life. What are your thoughts, emotions, and actions? How do they make you feel? What can you do differently to improve your life? By reflecting on these things, you'll be able to see things more clearly and make changes that will lead you to a more balanced and fulfilling life.

Visualization

Another great way to achieve turiya is to practice visualization. Take some time each day to sit quietly and imagine yourself in a state of complete harmony. Visualize that your mind and body are in perfect balance. See yourself surrounded by light and love. Fill yourself with positive energy and let it flow out into the world. By visualizing these things, you'll be able to bring them into your life and achieve a higher state of consciousness.

Prayer

Prayer is another powerful tool to help you achieve turiya. This means taking some time each day to connect with a higher power and ask for guidance. Pray for strength when you are feeling weak, courage when you are afraid, and wisdom when you are making choices. By praying for these things, you'll find them in your life and achieve a higher state of consciousness.

Connect with Nature

One of the best ways to achieve turiya is to connect with nature. Make time in your busy daily schedule to appreciate the beauty of the world around you. Notice the colors, smells, and sounds of nature. Feel the wind on your skin and the sun on your face. Take a deep breath and let the fresh air fill your lungs. By connecting with nature, you'll find balance in your life and achieve a higher state of consciousness.

Spend Time with Loved Ones

Spending time with loved ones is another great way to achieve turiya. This means taking some time each day to appreciate the people in your life. Talk to them, laugh with them, and just enjoy their company. Let them know how much you care about them. By spending time with loved ones, you'll find balance in your life and achieve a higher state of consciousness.

Be Grateful

Last but not least, be grateful for what you have. This doesn't mean that you should be content with your current situation, but it does mean that you should appreciate the good things in your life. By being grateful, you'll be able to attract more positive energy into your life and find balance and harmony.

Daily Recommendations

The previous chapter outlined a daily plan for achieving turiya. It's essential to have a daily routine that will help you stay on track. Here are some daily recommendations to help you get started:

1. Meditate for at least 10 minutes each day.

2. Make time for yourself to do things that you enjoy.

3. Eat healthy, whole foods.

4. Exercise regularly.

5. Get enough sleep each night.

6. Practice self-reflection.

7. Visualize yourself in a state of complete harmony.

8. Prayer for guidance.

9. Connect with nature.

10. Be grateful for what you have.

Achieving Turiya requires a lifestyle change dedicated to mindfulness and self-awareness. This can be a difficult process, but it is essential for reaching Turiya. The first step is to become aware of your thoughts and emotions. Be mindful of what you are thinking and feeling throughout the day. Pay attention to your reactions to situations and people. Notice when you are feeling stressed, anxious, or angry. These are all indications that your mind is not at peace.

The second step is to start making changes in your life to promote peace and relaxation. Begin by meditating for at least 10 minutes each day. Focus on your breath and let all other thoughts pass through your mind without clinging to them. Make time for yourself to do things you enjoy and make yourself feel good. This could include reading, spending time in nature, or practicing yoga.

The third step is to begin making changes in your diet and lifestyle. Eat healthy, whole foods that will nourish your body and mind. Avoid caffeine and alcohol, which can increase anxiety and stress levels. Exercise regularly to release tension and promote relaxation. Get enough sleep each night so that you feel rested and rejuvenated.

By following these steps, you'll be well on your way to achieving Turiya. Remember, it is a journey, not a destination. Take each day one step at a time, and be patient with yourself. Above all, enjoy the process.

Conclusion

In Hinduism, atman is the concept of the self, and turiya refers to the highest state of consciousness. In this state, the individual self is united with the absolute self. Turiya is a Sanskrit word meaning "the fourth" or "the highest." It is also known as pure consciousness, absolute consciousness, or the transcendental self. According to Hindu philosophy, there are four states of consciousness: waking, dreaming, deep sleep, and turiya. Turiya is the highest state of consciousness, in which the individual self is united with the absolute self. In this state, there are no distinctions between the subject and object, and all dualities are dissolved.

Many paths lead to turiya, such as yoga, meditation, and pranayama (breath control). Yoga is a system of physical and mental practices that originated in India. Meditation is a practice that allows the mind to become still and focused, and pranayama is a breathing technique that helps to control the breath. Mantras and mudras are also useful tools for inducing turiya. Mantras are sacred sounds believed to have spiritual power, and mudras are hand gestures often used in yoga and meditation. Yoga sequences can also be used to unlock turiya. These sequences are designed to open the energy channels in the body and prepare the mind for meditation.

There are many daily steps that you can take to move closer to turiya. Practicing yoga and meditation regularly is one of the best ways to achieve this state. Other steps include eating a healthy diet, spending time in nature, and connecting with like-minded people. By taking these steps and making a commitment to your spiritual practice, you can begin to experience the joy of pure consciousness.

Turiya is a state of pure bliss, peace, and unity. It is the highest state of consciousness that a human can experience. When you attain turiya, you'll feel a deep sense of connection to all that is. You'll also feel a sense of peace and well-being that is beyond words. This easy-to-follow guide helped you understand turiya and how you can experience it for yourself. It offered a step-by-step roadmap to help you understand this elusive but highly sought-after state and practice it in your life. Whether you're looking to improve your meditation skills or simply seeking more peace, clarity, and joy in your day-to-day life, this guide showed you how to find the inner stillness that lies at the heart of turiya. With just a little bit of time and effort, you can enjoy all the benefits of this timeless state for yourself.

Now that you have this knowledge, it is up to you to take the next step on your journey. Remember, the path to turiya is unique for everyone. Trust your intuition and follow your heart. And most importantly, enjoy the journey!

Here's another book by Mari Silva that you might like

MARI SILVA

EGUN

THE ULTIMATE GUIDE TO
ANCESTRAL VENERATION, SPIRIT GUIDES,
ODUN EGUNGUN, REINCARNATION,
AND YORUBA SPIRITUALITY

Your Free Gift
(only available for a limited time)

Thanks for getting this book! If you want to learn more about various spirituality topics, then join Mari Silva's community and get a free guided meditation MP3 for awakening your third eye. This guided meditation mp3 is designed to open and strengthen ones third eye so you can experience a higher state of consciousness. Simply visit the link below the image to get started.

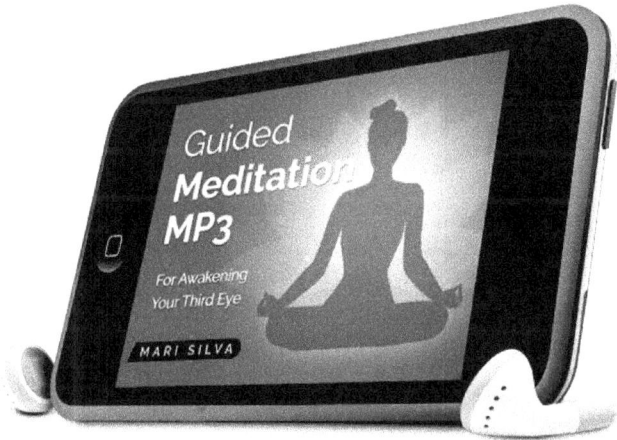

https://spiritualityspot.com/meditation

References

Borohhov, D. (2011, May 28). Turiya meaning. Ananda. https://www.ananda.org/yogapedia/turiya/

Chitrapuri. (2012, February 25). Shiva and Shakti. Chakras.net. https://www.chakras.net/yoga-principles/shiva-and-shakti

Darecki, Y. (n.d.). Turiya. Com.au. http://yogananda.com.au/g/g_turiya.html

Durand, K. W. (2008). Turiya: A Collection of Wordizms. AuthorHouse.

Hughes, A. (2020, January 29). Shiva and Shakti: The divine energies within us all. Yogapedia.com; Shiva and Shakti: The Divine Energies Within Us All. https://www.yogapedia.com/shiva-and-shakti/2/6052

Purohit, T. (2022, February 3). Shiva and Shakti - the divine union of consciousness and energy. TemplePurohit - Your Spiritual Destination | Bhakti, Shraddha Aur Ashirwad. https://www.templepurohit.com/shiva-shakti-divine-union-consciousness-energy/

The. (2017, August 7). Turiya: The fourth dimension of being. The Tribune India. https://www.tribuneindia.com/news/archive/lifestyle/turiya-the-fourth-dimension-of-being-448113

The Editors of Encyclopedia Britannica. (2021). samadhi. In Encyclopedia Britannica.

Turiya of the fourth state. (n.d.). Sivanandaonline.org. https://www.sivanandaonline.org/?cmd=displaysection&section_id=752

VivekaVani [VivekaVani]. (2021, March 25). Turiya in Vedanta - Pravrajika Divyanandaprana. Youtube. https://www.youtube.com/watch?v=2LIxwolSDJw

www.ingramcontent.com/pod-product-compliance
Lightning Source LLC
Chambersburg PA
CBHW071902090426
42811CB00004B/712